NOT JUST WORDS

HOW A GOOD APOLOGY MAKES YOU BRAVER, BOLDER, AND BETTER AT LIFE

DONNA MORIARTY

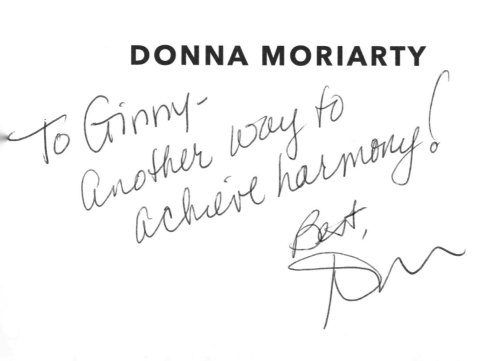

To Ginny—
Another way to
achieve harmony!

Best,
Donna

ISBN: 978-0-99958-120-9 (print)
ISBN: 978-0-99958-121-6 (ebook)

DEDICATION

To my husband Michael, my lifelong partner in love and forgiveness.

To my mom, who was my first reader and rave reviewer.

And to my amazing children, Zack, Ethan, and Amanda, for turning out so well in spite of my many mistakes.

CONTENTS

APOLOGIA

It happens every day, to all of us. We say or do something we regret. We feel remorse. We know we should face our mistakes and try to fix them if we can. In fact, there's usually a do-over window, a period of time when we can go back and set things right. But, whether because of shame or ignorance, we let those moments pass, and we're left with our uncorrected faults, crimes, and misdemeanors intact, with only a cringe-worthy memory to show for it.

In my years as a writer and editor, I've learned to accept, even venerate, the human need to revise. It's almost inevitable that our intentions don't come out right the first time. It's not only possible, but desirable, to go back and amend a first attempt that missed the mark. Often it's the only way to restore a damaged or severed connection or clean up the hot mess we made.

Of course, I'm not just talking about the written word. I'm talking about the ability to admit when we're wrong, and to do what we can to make it right.

Not Just Words: How a Good Apology Makes You Braver, Bolder, and Better at Life is neither a self-help book nor an etiquette how-to guide. It isn't about table manners or trying to be perfect. Instead, it is for those times when we blow it. By taking a few simple steps and facing what we've done with courage, humility, and grace, we learn not to be perfect, but perfectly human.

Let's have full disclosure here. I'm a baby boomer who wrote this book primarily for millennials. I can't tell you how many times I've heard people of the flower power generation bashing people of the post-Mario generation, calling them selfish, entitled, and surgically attached to their phones. We boomers are beginning to face the hard reality that eventually strikes at every generation—we're on our way out. Millennials are on their way in. And make no mistake, we boomers are skeptical about handing over the reins to millennials. We are exasperated by our experiences of dealing with the younger generation, whether at work, in our families, or in everyday life. We are shaking our heads saying, "What's the world coming to," sounding like our parents' generation.

But here's the great irony. Our generation installed the buttons that millennials are now pushing. We raised our kids to feel good about themselves and to believe they can do or become whatever they want in life. As for that much-maligned practice of giving everyone a trophy—guilty as charged.

What we didn't foresee were the side effects we were foisting upon our young: failure to launch, faulty manners, and a declining ability to relate to other human beings gracefully and effectively in real time and face to face.

Well, ready or not, the torch is about be passed to a new generation. If boomers have a legacy to pass along with that torch, it ought to be one of valuing human connection. With ice caps melting and hate speech on the rise—not to mention the siren song of omnipresent technology—it's never been more important and more urgent to understand human connections.

This book is not just for non-apologizers and the people who love them. This book is for everyone who wants to preserve and protect those human connections, which are the quintessential heart of what will save our world.

INTRODUCTION:
WHO, ME? APOLOGIZE?

The ability to deliver a good apology is a great, untapped power that lives inside all of us. If you can admit when you're wrong and follow a few simple steps to making things right, you will find yourself in possession of a subtle superpower that can transform your life, your relationships, your future, and maybe even the world. While admitting mistakes may seem like a sign of weakness and a surefire way to ensure that others will try to walk all over you, the opposite is true.

A heartfelt apology acknowledging the harm done to another, along with an equally heartfelt intention to repair any damage and make things right, is a little-known strength that lies in each one of us. It is a muscle waiting to be flexed, a tool for both building and repairing, and a healing modality that can deepen the bonds between humans and correct a lot of what's wrong with the world.

Not many people are going to get this. It's counter-intuitive, arcane, and a little old-school. But if you're reading this, maybe it's something you've thought about or even practiced. Either way, a spark inside you understands that, in a world where some people hardly look up from their phones long enough to make eye contact much less relate to each other on a deeper human level, there's got to be a better way.

A good apology well-delivered is an unexpected approach that differs vastly from the prevailing climate of me-first and sorry-not-sorry. The ability to apologize well is a skill, neither hard to learn nor to practice. Well, not once we get over ourselves, that is. A sincere and simple apology, which has roots far back in history and often gets lumped together with rules about which fork to use, is becoming a lost art.

Not many people are willing to honestly acknowledge a screw-up, figure out a way to make it right, and then carry out the plan. But those who have this level of courage and humility find that it sets them apart. I like to call them the spiritual one percent. Why bother apologizing when conflict arises? Why not meet the attack with your best defense to score the win? Why not crush your enemy and grind them into dust? I'll tell you why. Because the moral high ground has intrinsic value that we can never experience without choosing it. When humans start racing for the behavioral bottom, there is no end to how ugly and vile we can become. The only way to fight against the negative drain-swirl is to stop the madness, one person at a time. The key is to do the right thing, even if it means being shot down. Even if no one else is doing it. Even if you lose some things along the way, such as a bad job, a bad relationship, or bad friends.

In business this trait is called leadership. In spiritual communities, it's called moral fortitude. In relationships, it's called give and take. Being transparent, humble, and willing to fix what you broke gives you the opportunity to display courage, integrity, and trustworthiness. People will be drawn to you because they know where they stand. They feel steady and positive around you. If the laws of karma are true, you'll attract good things—more love, less stress. Saying "I was wrong" takes great courage because you never really know what the other person is going to do or say. They might use it against you or hold it over you.

But what usually happens is connection. When someone apologizes, everyone slows way down, gets very still and becomes totally present. They listen intently. Most people sense that a sincere apology is an experience that comes along rarely in life, and they don't want to miss a thing. Human interaction doesn't often go to this level, so when it does, everyone notices the difference. It's like spotting an ivory-billed woodpecker. Sensing the rarity and significance of the moment, most people will rise to the occasion, giving a fair hearing to the person who brought it to their doorstep.

You can be that rare, valued person. If you're reading this book, it's likely you already are.

Ready to make your little corner of the world a lot better?

Let's go.

PARt one

THE HOW AND WHY OF
THE GOOD APOLOGY

———

CHapTer 1
FAULTS, FOIBLES AND FOOLISHNESS

———

WE ALL KNOW how easily humans screw up, make mistakes, and generally behave in a flawed, human way. There's no shame in it. Where we go wrong is in failing to remedy errors in a way that makes us whole again. What if there was a better way? Well, stick around. There is.

Stupid human tricks

Bottom line: people are human, and humans make mistakes.

The problem is not with the all-too-human thoughtless remarks, quick tempers, fender benders, and spilled beverages. The problem is that most people know only one way to respond to someone else's screw-up: they react with anger. They stuff it down, burning with resentment, or they lash out. Suddenly many offenses have occurred instead of just one.

The problem with most people who commit an offense, whether unintentionally or with malice aforethought, is that they, too, know only one way to respond: with guilt, shame, and a desire to avoid or transfer blame elsewhere. They react impulsively, trying either to shift the blame or pretend the offending action didn't happen. This causes the conflict to escalate and increases pain and problems.

Think of the last time you were in a supermarket, in line at Starbucks, or playing pool with friends and minding your own business. Suddenly, words are exchanged between your best buddy and someone at the next table. Or someone decides to cut the line because, clearly, he thinks he's more important than everyone else. (Who cares if he's got a train to catch?) Or, you relate a funny story about your girlfriend's teeth-brushing habits, and the next thing you know, she's giving you the stink-eye, and everyone else is looking at their shoes.

You've just encountered conflict, my friend. Or, to put it any one of a dozen different ways, a blooper, a blunder, a misstep, a failure to communicate. Everyone makes mistakes. You've been hearing this since first grade. "That's why pencils have erasers," the teacher may have told you, although if it was a hot day in late May, she might not have said it nicely.

"Hey, Mr. Clumsy, you spilled your juice. You should try to be more careful," your Grandma might have said when you spent the night at her house. No wonder you don't enjoy visiting Grandma so much.

"Hey, watch where you're walking, idiot!" is what you're more likely to hear nowadays. Or worse. Much worse.

What happens when you make a mistake that sets off a heated reaction? Like when you cut someone off in traffic, accidentally burn a hole in a shirt you borrowed from your roommate, or call someone out in a team meeting because it's time somebody did it?

Well, that depends. If you're like most people, you might try to get away with it. In traffic, this is usually easy; you just floor it and get gone. In a situation with friends, you might try making a quick excuse: "I didn't realize my cigarette was burning so low." At the team meeting, as your coworker sets her mouth in a hard line and emits clouds of emotional steam, you might sink down in your chair, hoping it will go away, a purpose best served by blaming your victim. "She deserved it. She *does* try to take over every meeting!"

By using this form of rationalizing, you're justifying your own behavior solely for the purpose of dodging responsibility for your actions. *You* know why you did what you did. True, you ruined the shirt, you embarrassed the colleague, and you endangered the drivers around you because you darted for that opening in the traffic, but hey, you were late, you were hungry, and if you didn't do it someone else would. Most people should recognize that, right?

While your motives may be clear to you as being a mere foible or an innocent mistake, others are likely not to see it that way. In our minds, we don't deserve blame; we deserve understanding, even empathy. Everyone makes mistakes, so others should cut you a little slack, right? After all, most of the time you're a really good person, thoughtful, considerate, patient, kind. You give money to people living in doorways, you call your mother on her birthday, you take your girlfriend out on your six-month anniversary, and you make a new pot of coffee in the break room after taking the last cup.

But as you're probably starting to figure out, everyone feels this way inside. Everyone feels like they are in the right, and that when they make a mistake, they're sure that mistake is totally justifiable. What do you do when you screw up, and the other person is *not* sympathetic or understanding or even nice about it, but instead reacts with anger, accusations, maybe even insults, demanding an apology or payback or both?

Tossing them a quick apology may fire them up even more. One way or another, depending on your relationship, the offended party is likely to punish you for hours, days, or weeks. You might even have made an enemy—all from a simple mistake. By learning how to admit when you are wrong and being willing to make things right, you can accomplish some amazing things in all your relationships. The ability to apologize well is a tool that will help you find more ease, more power, more respect, and even more love. Like a Hogwarts spell or the hands of a faith healer, the power to right a wrong sends down a shimmering cloud of confidence in meeting many kinds of problems.

We all know what an apology is. Feeling bad about harm we've caused is in our DNA. We also know how it feels to be on the receiving end of another's injury or insult. That knowledge, also in our DNA, gives rise to a feeling of empathy. When our words or deeds injure another, we automatically feel, well, sorry. Sorry that they've suffered, especially if we caused it. Empathy and regret are among the finest of human emotions, and expressing regret stemming from empathy is among the finest expressions of human decency. Yet not everyone, even veteran apologists, can always respond appropriately in the heat of a moment gone wrong.

So why is it so hard for some of us to apologize? We're going to get into all that, but for now, let's just break it down. Sincere apologies often occur after you've had a chance to look at the situation rationally and have resolved to follow the four steps outlined as follows:

Four steps to a good apology

1. Admit it.
2. Express it.
3. Fix it.
4. Change it.

Step one: Admit it. An apology starts with admitting you made a mistake and caused harm to another. Never mind that you didn't mean it, or the harm was nothing more than being late for appointment; an apology begins by facing the fact you've caused harm, not by pretending it didn't happen or wasn't your fault.

The most important part of any apology is to first admit that you've made a mistake, which may seem obvious. The evidence is right in front of you: a flame war, a sobbing lover, an angry coworker. But the admission is often the hardest part for many people. It's infinitely easier to see our own actions as situational and reasonable, and the actions or reactions of others as selfish and irrational. Human nature tells us to believe that we are innocent, or at least justified.

So what did you do? You broke a lamp, forgot an appointment, told a lie, took something that wasn't yours, betrayed a trust, violated a court order, made a mess, disregarded a law, or passed along an STD. You plugged in the wires wrong, and the thing exploded. You shouted angry words that you wish you could take back. You pressed send.

If you're still not sure how to recognize your part, use your Spidey senses.

Remember when you were little, and you screwed up in some way? Say you broke a window with a fly ball, teased your little sister until she cried, or copied someone's homework. If your first impulse was to hide the evidence and run away, ask yourself why. You weren't in trouble yet. Before it was even discovered, you had a feeling, an emotional experience that a friend of mine used to call, "that uh-oh feeling in your tummy." You probably still have that feeling from time to time. We humans have a built-in mechanism that signals us when something is amiss. Call it intuition, your belly barometer, or a gut feeling, this feeling helps us sense danger and trouble, and originates with our ancestral instinct for fight or flight. In the modern human, with no wooly mammoths to outrun, this sense still serves us well, alerting us to disturbances in the heart.

But hold on, you might be thinking. If I'm the perpetrator, why am I reacting as if I'm being threatened? Because we know deep down that our actions have consequences, which may include punishment or retribution. That, my friend, is your conscience.

The uh-oh feeling is your cue. Take a look at the situation. Many times it's patently obvious, like your partner sobbing, "How could you say such a thing?" Other times it's less obvious, like a strong urge to cross the street to avoid someone you used to be friendly with. Don't fear that guilty feeling of recognition! It will help guide you out of the mess you're in. Be brave, and look at what you did to cause the situation or make it worse. Sometimes it's as simple as asking yourself, "If there was an undo key, at what point would I have used it?" There it is. Your mistake.

Step two: Express it. You know what it looks like when you've messed up. You feel tension in the air. Faces are red with anger. Gazes are averted. Tears are flowing, or objects are flying. Whether the harm is committed against a person's physical body, material possessions, or spirit, we express our regret. We use our words. The most common words are, "I'm sorry."

Maybe you already want to back away from this. But wait, you might be saying, I didn't mean any harm! Maybe you were careless or distracted. Maybe you should have known better, but did it anyway. Or you just went along with what everyone else was doing, knowing in your heart it was wrong. Sometimes our motives are to blame, prompting us to take more than our share or defeat an adversary by any means necessary. Maybe you were just standing there minding your own business, but the fact remains that you're in hot water, and you need to do something about it. If the deed was unintentional, that matters a little. If you sit on your Aunt Sadie's antique parlor chair and it breaks, you certainly didn't mean to do it. But the chair is broken, the value of it has changed, and the chair—and possibly your relationship with Aunt Sadie—will never be the same.

No getting around it. The words are, "I'm sorry." Using these universally accepted words to express regret can work like magic. Conversely, the failure to utter these words can create a world of pain. I could fill pages with the other words and phrases that typically populate an apology. The words are important, and so is the feeling behind the words. We'll get into this more a bit later on, but the thing to remember is the thing you did.

I'm sorry I (state the thing you did.)
I was wrong.
I never meant to hurt you.
You didn't deserve that.
I wish I could take back what I said.
I'm sorry, that was inconsiderate.
Sorry, I really didn't think this through.
It won't happen again.
Please forgive me.
Can we start over?

Step three: Fix it. Offer to pay for the damage, make it up to the person, and repair the broken bond of trust. The words and intention of the apology go a long way toward making that repair, but the words don't mean anything if you don't take responsibility. Even if you mend the thing you broke, it's never going to be the same again. A good apology includes a promise to make some kind of repair.

Of course, it's scary. If we're talking about a mild fender bender, even the thought of your insurance rates going up is going to cause a little stab of regret. But a stab of regret and feeling remorse for the thing you've done means you're doing the right thing. Remorse is part of your payment for your transgression and part of the healing.

Your expression of regret could be simple, as in a work-related incident: "I'm sorry. I wish I'd thought this through before causing all this trouble. From now on I promise to bring the problem to you first, instead of going over your head."

If it involves costly damage, like the time I sat on a guy's glasses that he'd left on a chair, the right thing to do is offer to pay for the repair or the purchase of a new version of the damaged item. "Gosh, they're ruined. I'm so sorry! Here's my email address. Please, I insist you send me the bill."

If the offending behavior was egregious and personal, like cheating on your partner or causing a big drunken scene at your sister's wedding, you have a lot of work ahead of you. But it begins with feeling regret for what you've done and saying the words, "I'm sorry. Will you forgive me? I never meant to hurt you. It won't happen again."

Step four: Change it. Make good on your promises, whether the promise is to do better or to never do it again. Relationships are a long haul. You might feel like you're in prison, always watching and self-correcting your behavior, but we can all agree that to continue committing the same offense, even without ever apologizing, is just begging for trouble. And to keep offending after you've apologized is just low-class and hopeless.

But we're not there yet. Stick with me, and we'll walk through it together.

CHAPTER 2
WHO APOLOGIZES?

———

RIGHT NOW you might be thinking: Who in their right mind would make a regular practice of admitting fault and apologizing every time they transgress? I know of only a few such people, and I've been studying the well-crafted apology for decades.

The practice of making an apology is neither uncommon nor new. It's a practice that has stood the test of time, with roots reaching back centuries, yet continuing to flourish and thrive in the modern world. The custom exists in the world's great religions and philosophies, in the social and psychological sciences, in law and medicine, and even works of art. Let's break down a few of these cultural precedents.

Religion and philosophy

Judaism

The Jews have *so* got it going on with the good apology. We're talking Yom Kippur, the Day of Atonement, baby. To my knowledge, the Jewish faith is the only religion to annually devote an entire day to the contemplation of wrongs committed, for which the person apologizes, seeks forgiveness, both human and divine, and tries to set things right. Blogging for *The Huffington Post*, Rabbi Mark Wildes describes an approach to the practice of atonement. Called Teshuva, the practice is more than just ticking a box so that you can cross "atone" off your to-do list. Teshuva helps you become a better person. Wildes explains that while Teshuva is often translated as "repentance," it actually means "to return."

"Teshuva is not simply about guilt, or coming clean—ultimately it's about shedding those barriers that block our true soul, revealing our true nature, and returning to the most elevated aspects of ourselves," says Wildes. He cites the late Rabbi Dr. Leo Jung's easy-to-remember approach to Teshuva using the "three Rs":

- Recognition. I admit, both to myself and the other person, that I've done them wrong.

- Remorse. I don't just say the words "I'm sorry"; I need to feel it.

- Resolve. I commit to changing my behavior so that I don't keep repeating the offense.

Starting to see a theme here?

Catholicism

The Roman Catholic sacrament of Penance, commonly known as the confession of sins to a priest, acknowledges the human need to acknowledge and correct wrongdoings. Here's where Catholic confession takes an odd detour, as the practice is largely carried out in the confessional and in private reflection afterward. Following the penitent's confession of sins, the priest administers a penance, which is typically dispatched with a few prayers and the resolution to "sin no more." It almost seems too easy. In fact, the fundamental belief that Jesus Christ died on the cross to redeem the sins of all of humankind starts to look like a get-out-of-jail-free card.

Not so fast. Although I've never heard of anyone receiving penance that required making an apology or restitution to the person harmed, the law does exist, at least on the books. Straight from the Vatican, Item 1491 of the Catechism of the Catholic Church spells it out. "The sacrament of Penance is a whole consisting of three actions: repentance, confession (disclosure of sins to the priest), and the intention to make reparation and do works of reparation." The next point in the Catechism, Item 1492, adds that repentance should be driven by charitable motives, not self-interest.

Which begs the question: is a poorly motivated apology better than none?

Islam

From Wikipedia: the Qur'an describes the principle of Tawbah, or repentance, which, like the Hebrew word "Teshuva," translates as the verb "to return." Look up "Tawbah," and you'll discover it can mean retreat, return, or regret. Taken in context of the Islamic faith, the word refers to disowning behaviors prohibited by Allah and returning to obedience to Allah's commands.

> *In the Islamic theology, the word denotes the act of being repentant for one's misdeeds, atoning for those misdeeds, and having a strong determination to forsake those misdeeds. Because Qur'an and Hadith repeatedly mention and emphasize the act of atoning for one's misdeeds, Tawbah is of immense importance in Islamic tradition. For a Muslim, it is regarded as a major gateway to rectifying his or her life.*

Buddhism

While there is some dispute as to whether Buddhism is more philosophy than religion, its wisdom and beliefs are practiced by people all over the world, striving to grow in goodness so as to end the perpetual cycle of birth, death, and reincarnation. And while the practice of apologizing for wrongdoing is not explicitly spelled out in sacred texts, some Buddhist practitioners cite the concept of mētta, or loving kindness, as an implicit command to correct harmful behavior, either by expressing regret for the harm committed or resolving not to repeat the behavior, or both, to speed up the journey to Nirvana.

The American author and Buddhist monk Thanissaro Bhikkhu, does a neat job of explaining the concept in his article "Mētta Means Goodwill":

> *As for the times when you realize that you've harmed others, the Buddha recommends that you understand that remorse is not going to undo the harm, so if an apology is appropriate, you apologize. In any case, you resolve not to repeat the harmful action again. Then you spread thoughts of goodwill in all directions.*

This practice accomplishes several things. It wards off our tendency to, in defense of the ego, deny that any harm was done. It strengthens our resolve to avoid doing harm. And it forces us to pay attention to the effect of our actions, so we can change before causing more harm.

Sounds like an apology, right?

Twelve-step recovery programs

Choose any one of the dozens of programs of recovery from addictions and addictive behaviors and you'll find a great apology strategy. If the program is based on the twelve steps originally developed in the 1930s by the founders of Alcoholics Anonymous (AA), practitioners inevitably arrive at the requirement to apologize.

Here's the precise wording from *Alcoholics Anonymous*, otherwise known as the Big Book.

> *"[Step] 8. Made a list of all persons we had harmed and became willing to make amends to them all.*
>
> *[Step] 9. Made direct amends to such people wherever possible, except when to do so would injure them or others."*

While AA is not a religion, the widely used and well-respected program of recovery serves the function of a spiritual backbone to millions of recovering addicts the world over. Nobody understands the need for a well-crafted apology like AA. It's not just the methods and useful tips they use, not just the extraordinary commitment to the practice, but also the philosophy behind it. In a very real sense, recovering addicts know that their lives depend on the rigorous practice of all twelve steps because to shirk even one of them could spell a return to the addiction and the calamity that surely follows. The practice is undertaken with bravery and dead seriousness, and the results can be impressive. I'll delve into how to practice this form of apology in greater detail in Chapter 11.

Business and leadership training

Many brilliant minds and business leaders of large, successful companies are beginning to recognize that everyone is human, and humans make mistakes that sometimes cost billions of dollars and endanger lives. Rather than continuing to enforce higher standards of behavior, many are seeking a more practical approach.

A growing trend in corporate employee training is the inclusion of guidelines on the right way to apologize to customers. A noteworthy example is Starbucks, which uses the acronym LATTE (Listen, Acknowledge, Take action, Thank, and Explain) to guide baristas in handling customer complaints. Other companies send employees for empathic leadership training at a range of sources, from the venerable Gordon Training International to the Landmark Forum. A Google search yields many self-help books and ideologies from just about every field. What they all have in common is a focus on the need for leaders and corporate executives—or the average person on the street—to learn how to connect with the end user in a meaningful way. The first goal is to achieve customer satisfaction, but a close second is the ability to handle dissatisfaction at every level, and in either case to express genuine concern and remorse when the individual or the corporation falls short.

Justice and law

In the last couple of decades, the restorative justice movement has been quietly transforming one aspect of American jurisprudence. Based on the premise that merely convicting and sentencing a criminal leaves out the most important part of the crime—the victim—restorative justice addresses the notion that justice without restitution is unjust. Its proponents claim that victims of crime inevitably suffer in ways that cannot be rectified solely by winning their case. The invisible scars left by their ordeal can only be healed by a meaningful, personal gesture between the perpetrator and the victim—a face-to-face apology.

After conviction and sentencing, the victim is given an opportunity to confront the offender in a supervised setting, sometimes called a Victim-Offender Dialogue. Blogging for the *Wisconsin Law Journal* in a post called "On the Defensive: The need for restorative justice," legal expert Anthony Cotton writes:

> *Restorative justice is effective because it lets the victim speak directly to the offender, outside the intimidating confines of the courtroom. The approach humanizes the offender, which also aids in the healing process. It offers the victim a chance to learn more about why the crime occurred, and the victim can express directly how the offender's conduct affected his or her family and loved ones.*

The impact of a court-ordered apology is powerfully healing, even transformative, for both the perpetrator and the victim. Both may feel some relief, and occasionally the victim may even forgive the perpetrator. Some people believe that the practice can lead to social reform.

To sum up, whether you look to psychology, religion, culture, the laws of the land, or the manners and mores of human beings throughout history, you don't have to look far to uncover a multitude of sources all saying the same thing. Society relies on the notion that the individual is responsible for their actions and the consequences that may follow. Nothing less than the social equilibrium of the entire planet is at stake.

CHAPTER 3
HOW NOT TO APOLOGIZE

———

IF THERE ARE a million ways to screw up, there must be a billion ways to make it worse. The colossal screw-ups that go viral are beautiful exemplars that stick in the mind. Bad apologies abound. Sports figures, politicians, and corporate executives hire public relations spokespeople to protect the brand, not fix broken things like hearts, fragile egos, or levees.

We've all seen those big, splashy public examples that bystanders videotape, post online, and share with millions of viewers within hours, sometimes minutes of their occurrence. We've seen the politician, after being caught in an affair, first denying it, then attacking the accuser or the victim, then announcing he's stepping down to spend more time with his family. We've seen videotape of the wreckage of horrific accidents that leave dozens of people dead or injured. Maybe it was caused by someone falling asleep at the switch, or texting, or being drunk or high on the job. The company spokesperson gets out in front of the cameras and says, "We're cooperating with the authorities," but denies all responsibility and says little or nothing about the lives lost or ruined by the tragedy.

We've seen the CEO caught in a criminal scheme that damages the lives of the company's employees or their customers, running a huge Ponzi scheme or subjecting employees to sexual harassment. The CEO may deny or lie or hire an expensive lawyer and may even go to jail for a time. But will that CEO ever apologize? Not likely. Chances are if an apology is proffered, it's likely to be a lousy one.

Finding any kind of apology from a public figure that isn't in some way self-serving is a tough assignment. Granted, a public apology can appear to be sincere, but the court of public opinion can go either way. Yet, as a gesture of assuming personal responsibility, does an apology make anything better for any of the victims of the offense? Did the perpetrator make any kind of restitution in an attempt to replace, repair, or restore what was destroyed, not only for victims but in many cases for those around the victims?

A poorly motivated apology is worse than no apology. And when there is no apology, that is, no attempt to repair the damage or harm done, no acknowledgement of the deep hurt and chaos that the offense created for innocent people, the whole episode is so much worse for the victims.

SORRY EXCUSES

Athletic sorry-not-sorry #1

A security camera caught former NFL football player Ray Rice in the act of beating his girlfriend Janay Palmer unconscious in a hotel elevator. But it was only after the video showing the entire ugly episode went viral that he apologized—although not to Janay. At a press conference, Rice apologized to his fans, the team's general manager, the staff at the hotel, even to his teammates for the "distraction." Janay herself, who stood with Rice at the press conference, actually apologized for what she called "my role in it."

Athletic sorry-not-sorry #2

During the 2016 Olympics in Rio, U.S. team swimmer Ryan Lochte falsely reported that he and teammates had been robbed at gunpoint at a gas station. An investigation revealed the truth. A drunk and disorderly Lochte had damaged the gas station restroom, and an armed security guard had demanded payment for the damage. For a while Lochte was arguably the most hated man in America. Did he ever apologize? Well, sort of. He took responsibility for his "over-exaggeration," as he called it, and for his "immature behavior" in a televised interview.

Corporate sorry-not-sorry

A viral video showing aviation security officers dragging the bloodied body of a passenger off an overbooked United Airlines flight after he refused to give up his seat caused horror and outrage. The airline responded first by blaming the victim. When that prompted even more of an outcry, United CEO Oscar Munoz issued an apology, not for the treatment of the victim or the trauma experienced by witnessing passengers, but for the inconvenience of having the flight canceled. In the ensuing furor the ugly truth came out. In fact, the flight wasn't overbooked as United had claimed. The airline had bumped passengers so that crew members could fly instead. United's reputation and stock both took a major hit in the wake of the incident, yet to date not a single employee of the airline has been fired over the incident.

Celebrity sorry-not-sorry

It would be hard to find a celebrity who's apologized more than Justin Bieber. His well-documented bad-boy behavior—smoking weed, puking onstage, telling racist jokes, throwing punches at paparazzi, canceling sold-out concert tours—has been caught on cell phone cameras and shared virally across the Internet. In an effort to salvage his career, Bieber started apologizing very publicly. He appeared on talk shows, posted a selfie video apology on Facebook, endured a celebrity roast in which half a dozen comics skewered him for all his crimes and misdemeanors, and when his turn came to rebut, wrapped up with another apology. Finally he released a sorry-not-sorry song titled "Sorry." It's as if he's using the apology to pay his way to the next offense.

Political sorry-not-sorry

Former Democratic Congressman Anthony Weiner, who was repeatedly caught sexting until he was finally arrested, convicted and sent to jail, delivered a string of bad apologies with which he tried to wiggle out of blame, pander to his constituents, and flat out declare himself sick. Despite Weiner's many public admissions of guilt, the former congressman finally pled guilty to a charge of transmitting sexual material to a minor. Only then did he publicly apologize to the fifteen-year-old girl with whom he had exchanged sexually explicit texts.

White collar criminal sorry-not-sorry #1

Investment advisor Bernie Madoff, while under house arrest before going off to jail for committing the largest financial fraud in the history of the United States, sent handwritten notes to the neighbors in his apartment building, apologizing for the inconvenience of television news crews and gawkers clustered around the building entrance night and day. What about Madoff's victims, who lost their homes, life savings, and businesses to the tune of billions due to his schemes? Not a word.

White collar criminal sorry-not-sorry #2

Martha Stewart was jailed for her stock trading misdeeds. Not only was no apology offered from the doyenne of cooking, decorating, and entertaining, but she managed to turn her jail sentence into a public relations coup. Incredibly, her release in 2005 was met with a spate of apologies to her. One journalist even hinted that Stewart must be a better class of white collar criminal, since she was the only one to serve jail time.

CHAPTER 4
THE UNAPOLOGETIC LIFE

———

THERE'S AN OLD joke that goes like this: Two motorists, traveling in opposite directions on a steep and narrow mountain road, come head to head. The one-lane road has a steep drop-off on one side and solid mountain rock on the other. If they expect to continue on their ways the only choice is for one of the motorists to back up to the closest turnout, yielding the right of way to the other. The first motorist angrily stops his car and gets out. "You'll have to back up," he says to the woman in the second car. With a smirk he adds, "Because I never back up for a**holes." Putting her car into reverse, the second driver says, "That's okay. I always do."

Refusing to back up for anyone else—and viewing them as a**holes without knowing a thing about them—is a lousy life strategy. The person who never admits they are wrong, never backs up, and never apologizes goes through life expecting everyone to bend to their will. Maybe you've encountered someone like that. Not your favorite person, right? Regrettably, they are not uncommon.

Conversely, being able to admit when you're wrong and do what you can to make it right generates a completely different atmosphere. It frees up the flow. Like the motorist in the story who was willing to back up, a person who is aware enough to know when it's time to compromise, yield, or stand down is the one with the power. The other guy has nowhere to go. He's stuck with only one response, which is to get louder and angrier until he gets his way. All that's needed for both parties to get where they want to go is for one person to compromise.

The seeds of a new approach

A lot of the pain and struggle in life can be attributed to an unwillingness to give in. In the schoolyard, giving in may have felt wrong, like quitting, surrendering, or losing. This feeling doesn't leave us when we leave childhood. Just saying the words, "I was wrong" is incredibly hard for most everyone, nearly impossible for some. One definition of the word surrender is, "to lay down arms and join the winning side." If you've been living your life according to a "no apology" strategy—meaning, you'd rather walk away from a relationship or a job before you'd willingly admit you were wrong— well, how's that going for you?

Meet Dexter.

Dexter is smart and well-educated. He has a decent job, an apartment with a couple of roommates, and a girlfriend. But he can't seem to get through a day without getting into some kind of dustup with someone. He forgets his six-month anniversary of dating his girlfriend, and he can see she's hurt, but says nothing. In a meeting with his work team, he rolls his eyes until the team leader finally calls him out, and he tells the guy exactly what he thinks of him. Everyone is embarrassed, and Dexter now has a couple of new enemies at work. Dexter visits his parents for the weekend, but on arriving he announces he won't be joining them for dinner because he's going out for drinks with old school friends. He notices the crestfallen look on his dad's face, but says nothing.

Waiting in line at the DMV, Dexter gets frustrated and impatient. By the time it's his turn at the window, he takes out his frustration on the clerk. With a hard look and a smirk, she gives him more paperwork and sends him to the back of the line. He spends the rest of his afternoon trying to get in to see her supervisor so that he can lodge a complaint, in the hope of getting her fired. He never finishes the errand for which he originally went to the DMV.

What's Dexter's problem? He sees himself as smarter than most people, more entitled to life's benefits, and always in the right. When he is in the wrong, he thinks of it as an aberration to be tolerated, even forgiven, by the person he has wronged. Yet if the tables are turned, and he is subjected to rudeness, criticism, or inconsiderate behavior from someone else, Dexter fumes. He expects, and often demands, an apology, but he rarely gets one. His opinion of his fellow humans sinks even lower. Wash, rinse, and repeat.

Everyone but Dexter can see that the real problem is Dexter.

Is anyone in your life like this? Sometimes such people are unavoidable because we work with them, are related to them, or live across the hall from them. It pays to ask ourselves how we might feel being around someone like Dexter. Uncomfortable? Angry? Superior? Be honest. Sometimes having a rude, sloppy, inconsiderate friend can be amusing or even comforting, especially when we compare our lesser faults against theirs. But sometimes Dexter is us.

Adding insult to injury

I'm a big fan of analog watches, the old school kind with a dial and hands. I even have a few that you have to wind every morning, but most of them run on batteries. I used to replace my watch batteries at a clock repair shop in town. Inside were dozens of old clocks mounted on the walls, sitting on shelves or piles of papers, and all of them ticking noisily.

The proprietor was an older man who spoke with a German or Swiss accent. He never smiled, and when he spoke his words were short and gruff. I was friendly and polite, but he didn't seem the type for idle chatter. Over the years I had brought several old clocks to him for repair or evaluation, and he was my go-to guy for replacing watch batteries.

One day I brought in one of my favorite watches, a sweet, simple timepiece with a mother of pearl face and a black ring painted around the inside rim of the slightly convex crystal. The watch was unique and elegant, and I loved it. I decided to wait while the shopkeeper replaced the battery, and I watched him idly as he stood at his workbench surrounded by little boxes of tools and gadgets. He placed my watch on a press to hold it steady as he tapped the back cover to loosen it and expose the battery. Apparently distracted, he placed my watch on the press face up instead of face down. The steel hammer came down on the crystal, smashing it to shards.

I was stunned. He, too, appeared to be frozen with astonishment and horror, but only for a moment. He quickly swept away the bits of broken crystal and examined the watch. "It didn't damage the mechanism, only the crystal," he said in that gruff way of his. "I'll have to order a new crystal."

I was still reeling, too surprised and upset to even think straight, and all I could do was nod. There seemed to be little I could do. Becoming angry would only make it worse. I felt a little sorry for him. Clearly he was a proud man, and he was probably ashamed of his careless mistake. Give him time, I thought, and I left the shop. I thought about how I would graciously accept the apology I was sure would come.

A few days later the watchmaker called to tell me I could come in and pick up the repair. When he handed me the watch, my heart sank. He had replaced the lovely curved crystal with a common, flat one, and the black ring around the face was missing. It looked like a dollar store Timex.

"That'll be twelve dollars for the battery," he said. I stared at him incredulously. "You're charging me for the battery after you ruined the watch? It's not the same watch." His face hardened, and I felt a stone wall materialize between us.

His expression was stubborn as he said belligerently, "I didn't charge you for the new crystal or the labor. I replaced the battery like you asked. You owe me twelve dollars for the battery." His chin lifted defiantly as he spoke.

Still stunned and at a loss, I handed over the twelve dollars and lingered, waiting for an apology. None ever came. I never wore the watch again, never returned to the shop, and never really recovered from the hurt and anger of that injustice. It wasn't his mistake—whether through clumsiness or distraction—that I couldn't forgive. It wasn't even the loss of an object of great sentimental value that wounded me. His coldhearted refusal to apologize was what truly got under my skin. He pretended his careless mistake had never happened, a mental fiction that justified his charging me for the battery. An apology would be an admission of guilt, so his response was to sweep it all away like the shards of glass on his workbench.

My takeaway? I resolved to master the art of the apology.

Because I said so

As children we've all been told to apologize, often by a scary, angry adult.

"Tell your brother you're sorry for breaking his toy."

"I trusted you to come home on time. You're grounded until I hear you say you're sorry."

"Hey, you two, stop this fighting immediately! Cara, say you're sorry for hitting Ramey. Ramey, say you're sorry for pulling Cara's hair."

The problem is, none of us, not even the scary, exasperated adult, knows how to apologize well.

When I was growing up, I knew of only four ways to respond when I knew I'd screwed up in some way.

1. Lie. Before you're accused, before they even look at you.

2. Say the words "I'm sorry" fast, whether you mean it or not. Those words will save you from getting into worse trouble when you get caught. Besides, if you don't say them, some grownup will make you.

3. Feel guilty. Once the guilt goes away, you're home free, even if your victim is still mad at you. You can throw in a fast "I'm sorry" here too, sincerity not required.

4. If it was really bad, go to confession. Once the priest gives you absolution, you're in the clear. In fact, it's as if you never did it at all.

This lack of proper training, if you will, is rampant throughout our society. But it does no good to look to earlier generations, who were arguably even less skilled at the art of apology. If you know anyone who grew up during wartime or its aftermath, you might already be familiar with their stoic sense of right and wrong. This group doesn't talk about feelings. Survival during hard times instilled them with a sense of personal responsibility, sacrifice for the greater good, humility that bordered on self-effacement, and a prodigious work ethic. The Silent Generation, as they were called, were influenced by the wartime need for secrecy, "duck and cover" drills in schools, and a fear of being different, outspoken, or critical of the government. It's a generation that doesn't apologize well. An apology reveals too much vulnerability, which should be kept under wraps. Taught to respect authority, even when that authority is clearly wrong, the Silent Generation will almost never apologize to a spouse, a grown child, or an employee. They raised children who were to be "seen and not heard."

Fast forward to the baby boomer generation, who came of age in an era marked by dramatic changes in culture and attitudes. Raised to revere self-expression to an almost fanatical degree, some proclaimed "if it feels good, do it," and "it's okay as long as no one gets hurt." Child-rearing boomers tried to improve on the practices of their own parents, who were big on discipline, such as spanking, taking away privileges, and "giving them something to cry about." Boomers believed in reasoning with their offspring to enlist their cooperation, avoiding any punishment or rules that could damage their child's sense of freedom and individuality. Following the advice of child care experts like Dr. Benjamin Spock and Penelope Leach, boomers believed that insisting their children display good manners impinged on the child's freedom. They believed spontaneous expressions of "please," "thank you," and "I'm sorry" would arise naturally when their free-range children were allowed to experience the consequences of their actions.

How well did this work? Terribly.

I was raised by parents who never, *ever* said they were sorry. It didn't matter what the offense was, whether spanking the wrong kid or taking a huge bite out of your ice cream cone. They seemed incapable of admitting they were wrong, had made a mistake, or might not know everything. I resolved to be a different kind of parent, the kind who would raise her children to be free and expressive, who would answer every one of her child's questions instead of declaring, "Because I said so, that's why!"

Easier said than done.

To spank or not to spank

When Zachary, our first child, was about three years old, a neighbor came over for a visit. Martha was opinionated and pushy, one of those perfect mothers who had read all the latest books and owned all the latest child-rearing equipment and gadgets. Martha used to come over and dispense advice on how to decorate my home, find fulfillment, and raise my son. I hated her visits, which I didn't know how to stop because I had been raised to be polite. (In other words, I had no boundaries.)

During this particular visit, Zack must have picked up on my anxiety. As kids will do, he suddenly started acting like a brat, constantly interrupting our conversation, squeezing his juice box until it burst, overturning a box of toys and scattering them all over the floor. Then Zack did the unthinkable. He marched up to Martha's two-year-old daughter Hildy and gave her a push. The little girl sat down hard on her bottom and began to cry. Martha, unperturbed, went on nattering about something, but I was mortified. I had long suffered a paralyzing fear of being a not-good-enough mommy, and now my child was proving it.

I grabbed Zack by the arm and marched him into his room. I started scolding him in a hissing whisper so that Martha would not hear and judge my parenting skills in this heated moment. All I wanted was to get my son under control. Where was the funny, cooperative child he was nearly every other minute of the day? But Zack wasn't in the mood to co-sign on saving my parenting reputation. Thirty seconds into the scolding, he shouted, "I hate you!" Without thinking, I reared back and slapped him hard.

I'll never forget the look on his face. First his eyes went round, then filled with tears that spilled down his face in Amazon rainforest-sized drops. He regarded me with an expression of such hurt and betrayal that it took my breath away. I was ashamed of my misguided attempt to impress the neighbor with my good parenting, and then to punish him for my own failure. In that instant, I saw myself not as a disciplining parent, but as a schoolyard bully.

My remorse was swift and terrible. I fell to my knees, apologies spilling from me faster than his tears. I gathered him in my arms and rocked him, repeating, "I'm sorry. That was wrong. You didn't deserve it."

No one had ever modeled how to apologize to a toddler, but I figured it out. I asked my little boy for forgiveness, and he generously gave it to me. I kept my promise, and I never hit him again, not in anger, or to teach him a lesson, or because of my own disordered priorities.

PART TWO

THE GOOD APOLOGY
IN EVERYDAY LIFE

CHAPTER 5
HARD WIRED TO FAIL

———

WHY CAN'T WE just follow our instincts when it comes to apology behavior?

Humans, with our capacity to think things through and decide how to act or react, not only have the capacity to express remorse when our behavior falls short, but we can also display humility, grace, and compassion for our fellows. Yet somehow, leaving the decision about whether or how to apologize in the hands of our instincts doesn't appear to cut it. Hold on a minute, I hear you saying. I've got a conscience. I'm a decent human being and a good person most of the time. In fact, I've got a pretty good system in place, which consists of following my instincts, which is pretty much the same as my conscience.

Why isn't that enough?

Well, let's get all your concerns out on the table.

Won't apologizing make me weak? As we saw with the two motorists, when you're too stiff-necked with pride to ever back down, or even just step aside so as not to impede progress, that's not strength. That's being an ass. People who stubbornly insist that others behave courteously, while not holding themselves to the same standard, are saying, in essence, "Yeah, so I'm a jerk. Deal with it." The considerate motorist with the witty repartee is the strong one in this scenario. Ditto with the watchmaker. Refusing to acknowledge his careless, costly error gained nothing, but lost him a good customer. Did that bad energy and poor customer relations lose him any more customers, or even put him out of business? We'll never know. But someone with that kind of negative cloud over his head may wonder why it always seems to be raining.

What if the other person is wrong, too? News flash: the other person often *is* wrong, but someone has to go first. No progress happens if two people continue to point fingers at each other and wait for the other to capitulate.

What if it wasn't my fault? If you're carrying a tray of lattes and are suddenly startled by a loud noise, causing the lattes to go flying over someone in your path, scalding them with hot coffee, you are not at fault but you are responsible for the injury. Anyone in that situation would likely agree. The correct response is to profusely apologize, help clean up the mess, ask if anyone was hurt by the scalding hot coffee, and offer to pay dry cleaning bills.

As a much simpler example, most of the time when you step on someone's toe, you don't mean it, but you still say "Excuse me," or "I'm sorry." It's common decency. Only when we start to deconstruct the offense's cause and effect, looking for someone to blame and filing lawsuits, does the problem escalate. The bigger the injury, the more people (and companies) want to wiggle out of responsibility. We've seen how badly that can turn out.

In sum, it doesn't matter if it wasn't your fault. Master the art of a good apology, and you'll see benefits, no matter what the cause, but especially if you were the offender.

Isn't this just kissing up? A hasty apology may seem effective because it can deflect the other person's anger. Don't get me wrong. An insincere apology whose sole intention is to manipulate the victim, cover up true feelings of hostility, or move on quickly to get out of the hot seat are not acceptable uses of an apology. That *would* be kissing up. But a good apology, delivered with sincere humility and the intention to repair damage, is the real deal.

They'll have the upper hand! I'll never hear the end of it. Maybe you've had this experience—admitting you were wrong, only to have the other person hold it over you forever. In fact, they bring it up every time you have a disagreement. "Remember that time you ignored my calls and texts, and I had to stand three hours in the pouring rain waiting for you to pick me up? How do I know you're not going to do it again?" Some people are petty and unforgiving, and will never pass up an opportunity to remind you of your mistake. No matter how many times you've apologized, or how long it's been since the offending behavior was committed, or how patient you are when enduring this mild form of abuse, they just won't get off it.

You don't have to put up with other people's harping, nagging behavior if you've swept off your side of the street. There's a way to put an end to someone who's just in your face for no good reason, and we'll cover it in Chapter 13. You don't have to be anyone's doormat, especially if you've adopted this higher order of good behavior yourself.

Won't apologizing get me into more trouble—legally, professionally, or otherwise? That's such an important topic that we've devoted all of Chapter 13 to situations where it would be unwise, even dangerous, to admit a mistake. Put a pin in that one, too.

The fundamental attribution error

A fascinating theory of group psychology, called the fundamental attribution error, states that all humans have a built-in misconception that everything we do is right. The perception ranges from our way of doing things to our choices and point of view. When we make a mistake, we believe in our hearts there was good reason for it. But when someone else makes a mistake, we judge their character, not the situation. We attribute bad motives to what they did, like selfishness, greed, or just evil intent. We fail to account for any mitigating circumstances, of which we know nothing, of course. We not only fail to spot the flaw in ourselves, but we even get a self-righteous boost of adrenaline out of the conclusion. That rush might explain why the fundamental attribution error has survived eons of evolution.

Here's how it works. You head to the quick checkout line with fifteen items in your basket instead of the twelve items specified on the sign above the cashier. In your mind, it's a harmless little exception. Someone behind you in line may see it differently, though. Something like, "Look at that selfish, inconsiderate witch. Life is so unfair."

Maybe you have judged others for various infractions, like not answering texts, taking the last doughnut, or leaving a public restroom without spraying the air. When you do it, it's a small infraction, completely justifiable. But when someone else does it, it's a hanging offense. Social scientists studying this theory figured out that in our minds, as in our field of vision, we ourselves appear as hapless victims of circumstance, like a photo-bombed selfie. Other people seem as small and insignificant as ants busily plying their trade on an anthill. Who cares what motivates them?

So when I see you darting and weaving in traffic, I conclude that you are a selfish speed demon who cares little that you're endangering the rest of us. But if I do it, I'm a good driver who simply needs to get somewhere fast, just this one time. It's the "all about me" effect.

Even more fascinating is the psychological study used to test the fundamental attribution error. Scientists videotaped subjects in conversation from two points of view, asking subjects to speculate on the motives of the persons being observed. The control subjects viewing the scene in real time followed the assumption that I'm good and the other person is bad. But subjects who watched a videotape from the other person's point of view flipped their perspective, seeing the other person as being right. Even more surprisingly, these "reverse perspective" subjects even attributed certain character flaws to *themselves* as they viewed their own behavior on the tape.

Then, consider the anonymity factor. Humans are naturally a little suspicious, even hostile, toward strangers or perceived "others." Social media is rife with behavior ranging from crude to cruel, seemingly triggered by the shield of Internet anonymity. When we don't know the people we're flaming, and can neither see nor hear them as human beings, they become our de facto enemy, or at least a threat. Imagine this scenario: a slow driver ahead of you is making you crazy. You can't get around him, and after a few miles you're cursing him. Suddenly you discover it's someone you know, and you feel the anger quickly ebbing as you automatically give them the benefit of the doubt.

Conflict, that ancient human trait, seems to be hardwired into our genes, as is the tendency to meet conflict with resistance. Social media has changed our world in many positive ways, but we can all agree that the impact has not been uniformly positive. With the anonymity that cloaks online interactions, we've seen a greater prevalence of mob psychology, which is the scary craziness that occurs when a group of people unknown to each other turns ugly, even violent and cruel. In crowds where we are largely anonymous, and no one can be singled out for blame, this subtle psychological mechanism can bring out the worst in us. Conversely, connecting, relating human to human, can accomplish the opposite. When one person pulls out of the blame-and-defend cycle, the whole situation can shift.

CASE STUDY

One hot summer day I was driving in bumper-to-bumper traffic in midtown Manhattan, and running late. I was trying unsuccessfully to get across town fast. It just wasn't happening. I decided to get off the avenue and try a side street. In the next lane I saw an opening in front of a cab. I gunned it and slipped into the space in front of the cabbie, who leaned on his horn. Hey, this is New York, I thought, before throwing up my hand in a one-finger salute. I promptly got stuck at a red light, which turned green, then red again. The street was a parking lot. I had nowhere to run.

I sensed a presence at my window, and knew it was the cab driver. He'd gotten out of his cab and was standing outside my window, shouting and gesturing. My heart was hammering as I rolled down my window. Then something came over me and a little interior voice said, "What you did was wrong." I was suddenly calm, and knew what I had to do.

"Lady, what the f*** is wrong with you?"

Of course, I knew what he was talking about. It's one thing to cut someone off in traffic, but flipping the bird because he honked his horn is overkill. The furious cab driver began to deliver a tirade about women drivers, the heat of the day, the frustrations of the traffic, and his conviction that people like me ought to be banned from New York City altogether. I waited until he paused for breath.

"I'm sorry," I said. "I was wrong to cut you off, and super wrong to flip you the bird. I always feel terrible when people do that to me. I'm sorry if I ruined your day."

Like a punctured bike tire, all the air went out of him. He stared for a moment, then blustered, "Aw, it's nothing," and huffed back to his cab. The traffic started moving again. I was dizzy with relief. I felt like I'd broken the code.

All my life I had been afraid of standing up to people. As a confirmed introvert, I'm highly averse to confrontation of any kind. When tempers flare, words desert me. All those clever, righteous zingers only come to mind much later, as I mull the scene over and over in my mind. A single heated argument can torment me for days or weeks. What I learned from the experience with the cabbie was how a sincere apology could melt away a conflict. I felt like I was channeling Mr. Miyagi. "Go with the resistance. Lean into the blow and it cannot harm you." But it was true. The cabbie's anger left him completely when there was nothing to fight against. I was hooked.

CHaPTeR 6
LOVERS AND PARTNERS (DID YOU SERIOUSLY JUST DO THAT?)

IF YOU'VE EVER been in a long-term relationship, you probably know the precise moment when you realized the honeymoon was over. All your lover's little quirks, which were endearing just a few months ago, now drive you crazy. From the way they pluck their eyebrows and leave the hairs in the sink to the way they always throw their coat over a chair instead of hanging it up. Every coat. Every chair. No matter how many times you remind them. Everything is suddenly cringe-worthy. Petty annoyances have a way of turning into petty squabbles, and before long you're fighting a lot more. Hurtful things are said. Maybe you apologize, and maybe you don't.

Where a good apology really starts to look like a superpower is in the way it helps you recognize and try to correct even just a few of the thousands of little mistakes people make every day in their most trusted, intimate relationships. Whether you are in a serious relationship or still swiping faces on Tinder, with this skill you will know more about staying happy in a romantic relationship than half the population that knows only two phases, honeymoon and divorce.

All the tips in this chapter can apply to any close relationship. That includes family members, roommates, friends, and even coworkers.

To recap the four-step apology:

1.   Admit it. Acknowledge what you did was hurtful to your partner.

2. Express it. Be sincere, and the words will come. All-purpose words are, "I'm sorry."

3. Fix it. Offer to make things right. Ask them what they need, if you don't already know.

4. Change it. Work to improve your behavior and keep your promises.

What makes an apology to an intimate partner different from everyone else you might have harmed is a matter of degree. Living with someone turns up the volume and intensity of missteps. But with practice you'll see an increase in the ability to be honest with each other and the desire to work things out. Both of you want peace, love, and happiness, so at least you're on the same page. And you're a lot more motivated to meet each other halfway.

Pay special attention to the part where you ask if they need anything more from you to make things right. Some romantic partners really want a grand display, like two dozen roses or a nice dinner by candlelight. But be careful. Too many errant apologizers mistakenly believe that flowers or gifts are a substitute for a sincere apology. Uh, no.

I know a couple who kept moving in together, breaking up, moving out, and doing it all again. The last time they were living under the same roof, he must've gotten spooked by the Groundhog Day feeling he was getting. He stayed out all night drinking with his friends, coming in the door at 7 a.m. with an armful of flowers, which his furious girlfriend promptly stuffed down the garbage disposal. Our man had fallen prey to the mistaken believe that gifts are more important than the feelings behind them. So, be careful when applying the floral treatment. If in the past your significant other has indicated a belief that gifts are a sincere expression of contrition and affection, then you're golden. You are still better off saving the presentation until after you've apologized.

By the way, this applies to apology sex, too.

To repeat: first find out what they need from you, not just right this minute, but in the future, too. (Do you seriously want to go through this again?) You may have to be quiet for a bit after asking, or after a pause gently ask your partner to think about it. An offer to change is not something that happens every day. If they don't quite know what they want from you, help them out with one or more of these conciliatory statements.

"It won't happen again."

Sometimes you have to bite the bullet and commit to behavior you're not entirely sure you can carry out, but once you spell out how you know you hurt them, the promise to change often pops out with complete authenticity: "It was really terrible and inconsiderate of me to get so drunk at your brother's wedding. I spoiled his day and embarrassed you. I never meant to hurt you. I was only thinking about my own good time. I promise I won't embarrass you that way again."

"Can you forgive me?"

If your intimate partner is the kind who needs to hear these words, they won't be satisfied until you utter them. It may feel weird to say, "Will you forgive me?" as if you're in a bad trilogy or a church confessional. But, with a partner who is longing to hear them, these words can have an almost magical effect. They will almost always say, "Yes, I forgive you," and the hugging and crying can ensue. If you know that's what they need to hear from you, say it so the healing can begin. After all, it's what you came here to do, right?

"I'll try to be a better friend/daughter/brother/person."

If what you did was more than a one-time thing, such as taking them for granted, repeatedly standing them up or being late to important occasions, borrowing their stuff and giving it back dirty or ruined, or criticizing every little thing they do, then a mere promise is not enough. If you've never really been the kind of partner, sibling, son, or daughter they deserve, then my friend, it's time to change your ways.

In twelve-step parlance, this is called "living amends," which means doing everything in your power to turn over a new leaf and become a decent human being, respectful of the feelings and needs of the people who matter to you. Every day. In perpetuity. Rather than trying to be perfect, this is about aiming higher, and that's a lifetime gig.

For example, if your offense is being late for everything, you need to work harder at being on time, even if you only do it for the person who you've inconvenienced by your constant tardiness. Set alarms, prioritize, and make sure you're on time for the most important things first, like formal occasions and airline flights. Get better at life. You'll benefit as much or even more than the person you're making it up to.

Just remember, whatever damage you've done can't ever be truly undone. This may sound like bad news, but it's just something you have to accept. Though you might be forgiven, you might not be let off the hook right away. Even after you've done all you can to make things right, occasionally your relationship will go into a cooling phase. You may have to leave them alone for a while. Sometimes, especially when making amends to old flames, the best approach is to *never* approach them. Your restitution is to allow them to move on.

Whether you're dating or in a committed relationship, a good apology will help your relationship grow and flourish. If you're not dating, applying some of these tools to all your relationships might change that. If you can accept this, you can find peace and maybe one day, someone to snuggle with.

Bonus relationship tools

It's pretty sweet at the beginning of a new relationship. You're falling in love. You can't get enough of the other person, and everything they do or say makes you happy. Even their little foibles are endearing. You want to know everything about them, so discovering that they leave their soggy teabags in cups all over the apartment or sleep with a nightlight and a stuffed dolphin are like finding little treasures.

But sooner or later this gets old.

To enter the long game of relationship, you will need to improve your communication skills to a degree you've never known. Relationships are not rocket science, but believing that a healthy, happy relationship will always be as effortless as it was in the beginning is a misguided notion. To make love stay, you can't phone it in or save it for special occasions. Like having clean dishes and good hygiene, a relationship needs attention every day or it gets disgusting and unlivable.

First acquire a few tools. Tools are what you use to repair something that is broken, stuck, or needs to be put together, as in a new relationship, or put *back* together, like a damaged relationship. You want it to be sturdy and beautiful and to serve you for a lifetime. So use your tools. Make no mistake, these are advanced skills, the master's program of relationship.

The Five-and-Five

When you're in an argument that goes on for hours (or days), pick up the five-and-five. It can be a game changer. I wish I knew the couples' therapist who invented this communication technique. The five-and-five is a simple exercise to clear the air between any two people in a close relationship, but especially in a romantic relationship of some months' or years' standing. Try using this tool whenever things get heated or tense, whether you're silently simmering with anger or engaged in a full-blown shouting match. Here's how to clear the air.

1. When one of you "calls" the five-and-five, the other is bound to consent. You both stop what you're doing, find a quiet, private place to talk, turn off devices and distractions, and focus on each other. Choose wisely when you call for one. You may have to agree to do it at a later time, when you know you won't be interrupted.

2. One at a time, each person takes five minutes to state their case—to say what's bothering them, what the other person did that's pissing them off, and what feelings they're grappling with. The idea is to clear the air, not go on a tirade. You've managed to capture your lover's undivided attention, so don't squander the opportunity. Focus on your own feelings and try to speak in statements that begin with "I," which help the other person know how you feel, instead of "You," which tend to be accusations.

3. During each person's turn, the other person agrees to pay attention and not interrupt for any reason. The whole enterprise will

go south in a heartbeat if you insist on defending your actions or correcting your partner's recall. You'll get your turn. If the first person goes on longer than five minutes, there's no need to get worked up. Just notice about how long it is and make sure the other gets equal time, but under ten minutes each. More than that, and you've got a rant.

4. Now stop talking about it. Seriously. The agreement between you is to avoid the subject for at least two hours. Glance at your phone, so you know for sure when that time is up and stick to it. No last word. No snide comments. Nada. Move on to something else. Put some breathing room between you and the other person, and go about your business as if you weren't having a knock-down-drag-out fight just a few minutes ago. As the proverb goes, "Least said, soonest mended."

5. After two hours, you're free to take up the subject again. The interesting thing about the five-and-five is its amazing power to make the subject a lot less important two hours later.

After you finish, two things are likely to happen. One is that you're going to feel better. Often when we get the chance to explain ourselves or express hurt or misunderstanding to someone who is listening carefully, the healing starts right away. Maybe we just need to feel heard, or in listening to our partner we realize we had no idea they felt that way. Either way, the five-and-five changes your whole outlook and theirs too.

The second outcome is that those two hours of not talking about the sore subject tend to whiz by. You might even forget to keep the argument going in your mind. When the two-hour moratorium is up, you may find that either you don't feel as strongly about the subject, you have nothing new to add, or you're just tired of the whole business and okay with moving on. Whether or not you resolved anything doesn't seem to matter now that you've put some distance around the problem. It usually doesn't seem worth getting back in the ring for another round.

When my marriage got to about year ten, we were having typical marital problems, fighting over money, kids, expectations, and emotional wounds, both intentional and accidental. The problem was not that we weren't suited for each other because we truly were. But we had no skills for overcoming these flashpoints. We started using the five-and-five for everything from simmering displays of passive aggression to full-blown screaming matches. When we faithfully followed the rules, it worked. We stayed in communication. We stayed in relationship. We stayed married.

More tools. More skills.

Agree to disagree. This is a great technique to use when the conversation starts going around in circles. It works well in games of poker, RISK, or D&D, especially when under the influence of alcohol and weed. One of the two parties simply says, "I think we should just agree to disagree." Once spoken aloud, these words can have an almost magical effect. You are, in effect, calling a truce that allows each person to retain ownership of their opinion without feeling the need to force the other to adopt their opinion. When you think about it, that's only fair, right? Because seriously, does *anyone* like being told they are wrong and that they should adopt another's version of what's right? Hands? I thought so.

Call a moratorium. This is the two-hour rule of the five-and-five, but without the five-and-five. It's great for those times when you don't have the luxury of sitting down and hashing out what's bothering you. In the driveway of the in-laws as you're arriving for Thanksgiving weekend is a great time to call a moratorium. Later you can agree to do a five-and-five, hopefully in the privacy of your guest room. If you are all sleeping in a tent in the wilderness, you're better off with agreeing to disagree. You can also call a shorter moratorium, but beware of the tendency to pick up the argument where you left off if you haven't left enough time to cool off.

Act as if. You've heard about this one, right? That's when you change your frame of mind by acting as if you really felt that way, like there's nothing wrong between you. You're not exactly faking it, but you are, sort of. Acting your way to right thinking is a lot easier and more effective than trying to think your way to right acting.

Try repeating a mantra. You can use "om" or "peace" or "nam myoho renge kyo," or even "How important is it?" If you're already practicing meditation or some other form of spirit-soothing activity like yoga or rock climbing, go for it. Anytime you take a timeout, putting distance between yourself and your own steamy emotions, you're protecting your partner and yourself.

Can you hear me now?

You're in a typical argument with your significant other. You try staying calm, reasoning, and listening. After a couple of days, the argument has been festering and growing to such a degree that you have no tolerance for anything the other person is doing. All communication ceases except clipped statements about who's picking up the dry cleaning and what time they'll be home for dinner because anything else threatens to spark the next big explosion.

Any escalating conflict will eventually spin out of control if someone doesn't intervene. It might manifest as a slow-growing disaffection with your partner that eventually convinces you that a breakup is the only solution. It may show up as a cold silence lasting for weeks, or a fast-moving fire that ends in violent behavior.

You need to get out in front of it before one of you passes the point of no return.

They say it's easier to get out of a burning building as soon as you smell smoke, instead of waiting until the flames have reached the third floor. Do that. Learn to recognize when you feel yourself reaching the red zone. If you recognize the other person approaching their red zone, call an immediate halt to the conversation and cool off before trying to fix what went wrong. You'll save a lot of heartache later on, not to mention a few dozen apologies.

CHАPTЕR 7
THE GOOD APOLOGY AT WORK

YOU'VE SCREWED UP at work. What do you do?

1. Hide it.
2. Lose sleep.
3. Worry constantly about being found out.
4. Create a plausible excuse in case your supervisor asks.
5. Avoid blame at all costs.
6. Tell your supervisor what you did and offer to make it right.

Anyone circle number six?

A sincere apology is the Swiss Army knife of the human behavior wilderness. It can mend rifts, heal wounds, and repair damage inflicted on a material object, a reputation, or a relationship.

CASE STUDY

Marisol loved her high-level public relations job at a university, having climbed the ladder from magazine editor to head of communications. Many times during her fifteen years there, she had navigated the administration's love-hate relationship with one of its donors, a large nonprofit. Part of her job involved protecting the university's relationship with this donor. When the two institutions found themselves on opposite sides of a hot-button issue,

Marisol, believing that transparency fosters trust, made her case to the executive leadership about issuing a press release that would present both sides of a sensitive issue the two institutions were grappling over.

As soon as the press release hit the media, Marisol's boss, the university president, got a phone call from the CEO of the nonprofit. They felt betrayed and set up. "We're out," the nonprofit CEO declared to the press. Rumors swirled about the impending dissolution of the partnership. When Marisol's boss told her the news, he didn't pull any punches. "We never should have issued that press release," he told her. "It was a bad call."

Marisol felt the color drain out of her face. "It was my call, sir," she managed to say. "I'm responsible for that communication. I misjudged the situation and made a recommendation that backfired."

She hesitated, knowing her error was costly. Her leadership training came to the fore. "If you need a sacrifice, I'm willing to be the one." She surprised herself. Wait, did I just offer to be fired over this? Then she thought, well yes. It was my mistake, even though others had approved it. She didn't want to lose her job, but she also didn't want the rest of her career haunted by doubts about her ability or her professionalism. She decided on the ultimate gesture of integrity: falling on her sword. Her boss looked at her for a long moment, then said, "It's bad, but there's no need for a beheading." He asked Marisol for a proposal outlining ways to repair the rift, and she promised he'd have it by the end of the day.

In the ensuing weeks, the entire executive team worked together to fix the problem, factoring in Marisol's new recommendations. The crisis was averted, and Marisol, wiser by far, humbled by her mistake, and grateful for the support she received from her employer, felt she was a more valued employee.

Apologizing at the office

There's a lot of talk these days about being a team player, creating a positive company culture that levels the playing field, and giving everyone a sense of contributing to the company mission. But hidden under that feel-good froth are ordinary people behaving the way they've always behaved since the industrial revolution: throwing coworkers under the bus, telling tales to the boss, and stepping on anyone who gets in their way. Okay, not always. Not everywhere. Not you, of course. But can you honestly say you've never witnessed crappy behavior in the workplace? What happens when someone admits they've made a mistake at their job? Your first thought might be, well, they get fired. Not necessarily. In fact, not usually. Instead, they come across as professional, ethical, and courageous. A leader.

When I had a corporate manager's job, reporting to the CEO, I always tried to be kind and courteous to the administrative assistants, the payroll clerks, and anyone with a thankless job. These workers are the backbone of any organization. Trust me, you need to cultivate their good will if you want to get anything done.

A guy named Roy worked in the accounting department. I won't lie; I didn't like him. Roy seemed to really enjoy jerking my chain. He routinely withheld information, would take forever to provide numbers I asked him for, and always waited until my third or fourth email before replying. You may have encountered this: someone with a little power who enjoys rubbing it in your face and holding it over you like a weapon.

Finally we had a showdown. I needed some data from Roy to complete a report that was due on the CEO's desk the next day. When I called him to ask when I would have the figures I needed, Roy informed me I would have to wait for, oh maybe a week or so. I'd had enough. Through clenched teeth, I said, "Let's hope it goes more quickly than that. I'd hate to have to tell the CEO that his proposal got stuck here on your desk." Roy blustered, "These things can't be rushed. You're not the only person we serve." Of course, no report showed up on my desk the next morning, but something else did: a note from human resources.

Apparently in HR-speak, my remark to Roy was viewed as a threat, a huge workplace no-no. I had thrown around the weight of my position to imply consequences that I had no right to threaten—tantamount to harass-ment. The human resources director recommended that I apologize to Roy, "so there are no unintended consequences of your action."

When you owe someone an apology, it's a lot better to arrive at this conclusion on your own than having it forced on you by someone who could eat your lunch. Nevertheless, I knew the HR director was right. I had brought the trouble on myself when, in my frustration, I had implied that Roy's job was in jeopardy if he didn't hop to the task I'd given him. I swallowed my pride, went to Roy's cubicle and knocked on the frame. He'd been expecting me. I apologized for misusing my position to manipulate him. I thanked him for the job he did. "You work hard and have a lot of conflicting priorities, and I was just trying to muscle my way to the top of the pile," I said. "It won't happen again." Then I added, "I'll take the report whenever you can get to it, but it has no bearing on you or your job."

I stole a glance at Roy. He was looking at me in astonishment. That's one of the magical things that can happen when you apologize. Whatever they thought of you before, your display of humility and good will changes something. It enables them to see the decent, helpful, hardworking you. It's a paradoxical superpower.

If a humble apology can have this much impact on a single conflict, imagine what it can do toward putting you on good terms with every per-son at your workplace, not just the people with whom you work directly, but also the clients or customers you serve. Imagine being able to walk a little taller, with a little more confidence and integrity. When you're not shrinking in fear of your own human fallibility, unafraid of taking respon-sibility for your misses as well as your hits, you start to look like a leader, someone who's fully invested in the organization. You might even start to like your job.

The fact is, the world loves people who can admit when they're wrong. I use the word "love" intentionally. If you look into the face of the person to whom you've apologized, you'll see it. Their expression is relaxed and full of wonder. No anger, no resistance.

The greatest peacemakers throughout history were not perfect. They were ordinary human beings trying to make a better world by being the change they wanted to see.

CHAPTER 8
FRIENDS AND FRENEMIES

———

RIGHT ABOUT NOW, you may be asking yourself, why should I bother? Do I really want to be someone who is good at admitting I'm wrong? What kind of person does that? The wimpy kid, that's who! I'll be the whole world's bitch! I'll never have the life I want.

Calm down. It's not that horrible. The person with a good apology in their back pocket is worthy of respect. They can be trusted to do the right thing. They have developed that sixth sense, the belly barometer. When they encounter a problem, they scan their behavior to see their part, do what must be done, and move on. They—or you, should you decide to accept it—will discover that the rewards are great, and the results incredible, and you'll wonder how you got along without it.

On the other hand, the person who bulldozes through life taking what they want and never looking back to see the litter of broken relationships and burned bridges they've left behind them inevitably runs up against a whole lot of trouble. While they may become adept at coping, fighting, pretending, or running away, sooner or later their world starts shrinking. Relationships become more strained or more shallow. Dexter's life is a life with few choices. He keeps doing the same thing over and over, even when it's not working.

Mastering the good apology allows you to develop trustworthy instincts. You'll know how to transform angry people into cooperative allies, adversaries into friends, and disappointments into opportunities for greater closeness in all your important relationships. In other words, you'll be on your way to becoming the kind of person you always believed you could be. Whether or not you believe in karma, the Buddhist principle that governs the nonlinear way our actions determine consequences, it doesn't take an ascended master to recognize that a life of negativity and belligerence reaps negativity and belligerence in return.

But the person who stands tall and admits when they're wrong knows that life can be a sweeter ride. In essence, you're telling the other person they matter. And no one, not your mom, your boyfriend, or a stranger on the subway can ever get enough of that. There's that pay it forward rule, too. A person who has been treated well tends to treat others well as they go forward with life. The universe gives a high approval rating to that kind of behavior, repaying you handsomely with even more power and serendipity so you'll keep up the good work.

Marked spaces in the parking lot of life

My friend Lacey has gone through life driven by a mental image of her mother, shaking her finger and scolding. Though her mother has been dead for years, Lacey still feels the pressure of that wagging finger, and no surprise, she turned out to be just like her mother. Her husband, kids, friends, and coworkers have all suffered under her incessant criticism. It wasn't until her first grandchild was born, and Lacey wasn't especially welcome in her son's home because of her criticism habit, that she turned over a new leaf. She became willing to see and admit when she was wrong, and she decided to allow that humble strength to guide her life in a different direction.

Lacey called me the other day with a great story. She had driven around for ten minutes looking for a parking space at Walmart. Spotting one, she'd been about to back into it when she saw in her backup cam that another car was pulling into the space from the opposite direction. The other driver hadn't seen her, and Lacey slammed on her brakes just in time. She told me her first thought was, "Son of a bitch, this is my parking space." Her second thought was, "Well, I didn't get to it fast enough, so clearly it's not my parking space." Lacey pulled away to search for another spot, which she found quickly enough, and parked. As she was locking her car, Lacey was startled to see the driver of the other car approaching her. She got nervous. What did he have in mind? Had she done anything to offend him? She waited as he approached, and then stood astonished as he dropped the bombshell.

"I'm really sorry I grabbed your parking space," he said. "It was inconsiderate, and we might have had an accident. It's just a reflex action for me. I guess I'm an aggressive driver."

Lacey was used to apologizing when necessary, but she rarely found herself on the receiving end. She was struck by how differently she felt about the man now. His face looked kinder, and she noticed the briefcase and the tray of lattes he was carrying. She concluded he was someone who worked hard and did things for other people, and her heart softened.

Recovering her wits, Lacey assured the man there were no hard feelings, and they parted ways. But the good feelings from her parking lot encounter stayed with Lacey for a long time and fueled her faith that she was making a difference. Something about a deftly delivered apology feels almost like magic. Of course it's not magic, which is how we escape reality, but the opposite. A good apology requires us to be fully present. Maybe you've heard that expression, "Be here now," and wondered how to make it happen. This is how.

When you really *see* another person just as they are, and they really see you, you immediately stop that habitual thing we all do when we're skimming through life, barely noticing the flow of humanity that's happening all around us. Being fully present gives us a life that's richer and more intense. Life may taste sweet, or it may be peppery, but at least we are tasting it. Every day we all encounter dozens or even hundreds of other people, close enough to touch but never really connect, except in the most superficial ways. Once you've had the kind of this-is-for-real moment that Lacey experienced, you will crave more. Instead of avoiding people or constantly wagging your finger at them, you'll want to dive happily into the life that surrounds you. Instead of skimming along the surface, you'll know the exhilaration and confidence that lets you swim out to the deep end.

Fifty ways to ruin a friendship

Intimacy is not just for romantic entanglements. Intimacy grows with any bond that resonates with our deepest nature. It's the warmth and closeness we feel in our closest relationships. We can feel it with a friend, a lover, or a sibling. All intimate relationships can be destroyed through ignorance, selfishness, and the willful desire to be right. With the proper application of a good apology, however, intimacy can be restored.

If you're like most people, your tribe consists of the people with whom you feel most comfortable. Even with someone you've only just met, you can experience that tribal connection that makes you feel immediately at ease. You instinctively sense you can talk with them about anything, use your most potent curse words, and freely offer an opinion on any subject, because they *get* you.

But what happens when trouble arises in this paradise of like-mindedness? Say you express an extreme position on something, and their stance is slightly to the right or the left of yours. You want to argue your point. They feel comfortable arguing theirs. You both go on and on, each making your points. The conversation lasts for hours. Beers are opened. Visits to the bathroom become necessary. And, still the "discussion" drags on until everyone is exhausted. Still you don't feel satisfied, so you won't rest until you've convinced the other person to come over to your side.

What you thought of as an easy tolerance with your friend or coworker, a mutually accepted range of agreeableness based on how much you seem to have in common, has come to an impasse. Right now you may be seeing your erstwhile friend as misguided, someone merely in need of a little more information to straighten out, or you might actually be soured on the relationship. But if you haven't been able to convince them with your best material, then it's time to take a step back. What's happening is relationship damage, a rift in the making. Time to mobilize your apology first responders.

You can do this by looking at it from a different angle. Start by imagining that you might possibly be wrong, or that both of you may be right. Being wrong is not so different from making a mistake, although it falls short of doing harm if you don't take it there. Unfortunately, though, sometimes we do take it there, and we chalk up another broken friendship.

Remember the fundamental attribution error? If you could watch a video of the conversation, seeing yourself as small in the picture and the other person as large, how would that change things? You might listen to them a little differently. You might just agree to disagree. Accept the fact that, while you still believe in your own convictions, you're not going to convince them today. Turn your perspective around, and you might even see that it's you who needs convincing.

If you've decided you want more peace and connection in all your relationships, and you've started looking at your life from the point of view of "do no harm," this kind of awareness is vital. It should give you pause. We've all been in heated arguments, and it's really hard to pull up short. Even if you're not ready to apologize, you might think about saying something like this: "I feel pretty strongly about this issue. I think my passion may have blinded me to any other point of view. I hope I didn't make you feel like you were the bad guy, or that I needed to fix you. Your opinions are important to me, and so is our friendship. I'll try to be more open minded next time we disagree."

That wasn't so bad, was it?

CASE STUDY

Nathan found a great apartment that came with two roommates he'd never met. They all sat down to talk before signing the lease, and Nathan felt they made a good mix. He saw a few potential problems with Gabe, the pricklier of the two, but Nathan felt confident that all three of them would do right by one another.

Then the inevitable happened. Relations between Gabe and the other roommate, Sarah, grew first nitpicky, then distant, then hostile. Nathan's efforts to mediate worked temporarily, but the constant hostility in the apartment continued to spiral, making everyone miserable. When he discovered that Gabe was planning to bail on the lease, just to stick it to Sarah, Nathan started to panic. His parents had co-signed on the lease. If Gabe walked, Nathan's parents, who had acted in good faith for their son's interest, would be on the hook for thousands of dollars. The terms of the lease also dictated that Nathan, and not the other two, was responsible for finding a new roommate to pick up Gabe's portion of the rent and utilities, but there was an expiration date on that. Nathan knew it was critical to negotiate détente between Gabe and Sarah.

Nathan called a house meeting. His two roommates sat on the edge of their seats, as if ready to bolt. "You guys have to find a way through this," he told them. "We don't have to like each other, but we're in this together. If one of us decides to bail, we all suffer. If one of you decides to walk away from the lease it leaves the other two holding the bag, and that's just wrong. Look, you're both decent, smart, cooperative human beings. There is absolutely no reason why we can't work this thing out. I can't force you. All I can do is ask. So I'm asking."

Nathan got up and went into his own room, shut the door and put on headphones. He didn't want to hear what was happening between Gabe and Sarah, and he was sweating bullets. His worst fear was having to go to his parents and explain this colossal failure. They would never trust him again, and they'd certainly never be as generous with him again if he couldn't pull this thing out of the fire. He had done all he could, and it was out of his hands.

There was a knock at the door, and Gabe poked his head in to say that he and Sarah had declared some sort of truce. It was not as if the half-hour of talking, arguing, and soul-searching they'd just gone through suddenly made them buddy-buddy. Quite the opposite. Gabe had decided to move out, but knew of another roommate that might be interested. Sarah had agreed to seek out other possibilities in case Gabe's friend didn't come through. Gabe was willing to stay on month to month until the new roommate was found, and both agreed to limit their communication to the necessities, and they would be civil about it.

The six weeks that it took to find another roommate were awkward and tense as Gabe and Sarah circled each other like tomcats. It wasn't a perfect arrangement, and they didn't follow their own rules perfectly, but the situation went from DEFCON 2 to all quiet on the western front, and in the end, a new roommate took Gabe's place. A year later, Nathan ran into Gabe, who thanked him for showing it was possible to get through a volatile situation without freaking out or running away, or doing something he'd really regret one day. "You made me want to be a decent guy instead of a selfish jerk," Gabe told Nathan.

CHAPTER 9
SPLINTERS IN THE FAMILY TREE

———

WHETHER YOUR EARLIEST memories of your brothers and sisters, cousins and uncles, parents and grandparents were friendly and fun, fraught with rivalry, or utterly toxic, nobody seems to get through life without revisiting those family relationships in adulthood. Let's start with birth order. If you're the oldest, do you find you catch all the flack, while the middle kid gets to rebel and be independent, and the youngest gets away with murder? If you're the middle child, do you feel invisible amidst all the drama going on around you?

Let's move on to money and property. Maybe you have a grandparent who has died or is downsizing. Some of your relatives are acting like Grandma's house is a free Target store. Uncle Frank swoops in and takes the choicest pieces of furniture, plus the riding lawnmower. Your sister helps herself to a coin collection you always thought was yours because Grandma told you once that she really wanted you to have it. Some families come to blows over things like this, and often for much less.

Your mild superpower can help by enabling you to talk about things that families don't usually talk about. You can be the lead operator on this project. As with your friends, showing how it's done can often help, or even transform, a feuding situation. The key is to begin by sweeping off your side of the street.

Let's start with mom and dad issues. Say they're divorced, with new partners, and you just don't get along with them. Maybe you resent one or both of your parents for breaking up the family. Maybe you've spent years taking advantage of their generosity, only calling when you need money or a place to crash, and expecting them to clean up your messes, even though you're almost thirty. This can just as easily apply to in-laws, aunts, uncles, grandparents, and family friends of that generation who have held an important role in your life.

If this line of thinking causes you to have that uh-oh feeling in your tummy, it's time to bring out the four-step apology plan. Cue the recap.

1. Admit it.
2. Express it.
3. Fix it.
4. Change it.

Start by looking for any hard evidence that you've caused some harm, such as complaints from the parental units that you never call or write, or guilty feelings because you've missed a couple of birthdays. These are harms that fall on the mild end of the spectrum. On the spicy-hot end are shouting matches, cold shoulders, unpaid debts, words spoken in anger, and even theft or violence.

Your next task is to own your actions and recognize the harm you caused. Even if you're not a parent yet, you can probably imagine how it feels for a parent or family member who's been taken for granted or mistreated by a young person to whom they've devoted time, energy, and funds. Hurtful behavior, ranging from ignoring them to crashing their car, cuts deep.

Remember the goal is a clear conscience, a mended fence, the brave feeling that you can face any adversity if you can face up to your part. Now go to it. Write out or think through the words you think they need to hear. Think about your approach. Plan a special visit, meet for dinner at a quiet restaurant, or invite them to your home; all these are great ideas. Waiting until the next family function where you lamely toss off a quick apology with everyone else listening is not.

Once you have the venue, make your apology. If your crime was little more than benign neglect, your amends will often start something like this:

"I know I haven't been the best son/daughter to you. I've taken for granted all the things you've done for me."

Of course, if you've got a more serious offense to apologize for, you have to take the leap. Use your own words, with the following examples as a guide: "During my starving artist days, I let you bankroll a project that never really got off the ground. I'd like to pay you back the money you loaned me. It will take time, but I can pay you $100 a month until it's paid off."

"I was mixed up in drugs for a while, and I did some pretty bad things. I took money from your wallet, had parties in your house while you were away, and burned holes in your Chippendale sofa. I feel terrible that I did those things. You never deserved it. You've always tried to help me, even when I was beyond help. I want you to know I'm not that person anymore."

If you're in a recovery program, now would be the time to tell them that if you choose. But only if it's true, and you're serious about sticking. Offer to pay for any damage you've caused, being sure to get an estimate before you make your approach.

Always state your apology in no uncertain terms. For example: "I want you to know how sorry I am, and that I'll try to do better from now on." You can also try using this awesome closer: "What would it take to set things right with you again?" And then shut up and listen.

With a few variations, parents and other adults who've been important to your growth and development, such as teachers, older siblings or relatives, and maybe even your first boss, tend to react to this type of apology in very positive ways. The most common reaction is forgiveness, understanding, and generally lots of tears and hugging. Often they're so surprised and grateful to hear words of appreciation for all they've done for you, not to mention your commitment to making things right, they are satisfied with just the apology. What loving parents and other concerned adults want most in this world is simply to know that their charges have grown into decent, reasonably happy human beings. By showing them respect and appreciation for the truly tough job they've had in raising you, you tell them that it's all been worth their sacrifices.

You can finish up the conversation with the stated intention to do better, and seriously, try to do better. You don't want to be having this identical conversation in a year or two, head hanging as you beg forgiveness for the same behavior.

While the reaction is usually positive, a few parents and older adults may have a hard time with the whole enterprise, not because they can't forgive you, but because they aren't comfortable expressing such deep and complex emotions. If you're apologizing to someone from a generation that grew up keeping things close to the vest, what you might get is an indifferent wave of the hand. When I sat down with my own mother to apologize for my waywardness and transgressions on her goodwill, I wasn't sure what to expect. For years after I left home, I treated Mom like my personal assistant. I visited only when I felt like it, brought boyfriends into her house and made all manner of noise and commotion in the bedroom I grew up in, and never lifted a finger to help. For years I had seen myself as her darling. I presumed on her goodwill and love and allowed her to dote on me, giving me money, favors, attention and forbearance. Within six months of becoming a mother myself, I saw what a crock this was, and what a horrible daughter I had been.

But my mother didn't want to hear it. I swear I would have been discreet when talking about the boyfriends, but I didn't get that far. She literally waved a hand at me, as if to sweep away the cobwebs of the past. "Don't even mention it. It's water under the bridge," she said. I started to insist, and she became almost cranky. "I said don't mention it. It's ancient history." For days afterward, I was perplexed and hurt by her dismissiveness. I mean, didn't she appreciate how hard it was to approach her with this apology? Then I remembered that it wasn't about me. My intent was to make things right with her and repair our relationship so that she felt loved and respected.

To admit what you've done along these lines is to expose all your tricks, like pulling aside the curtain that's been hiding your less-than-admirable motives. Once the other person has peeked behind the curtain, you can't pull the same crap again. Making amends to my mom was just the beginning of a longer term goal of changing from a bad daughter to a better one, and that did not include the right to object to her way of responding. Instead of adding to my list of offenses by copping a hurt or resentful attitude, I honored her request, and we never spoke of it again. My relationship with her now is clean and authentic.

The bottom line is that some people may be uncomfortable with your attempt to set things right. It's intimate and a little embarrassing, and it can stir up the past. Be gracious and let them have their say. You're getting plenty of benefits from this exercise, namely freedom, a clear conscience, and new strength of character, whether or not the conversation goes the way you expect.

CHAPTER 10
SOMETHING TO BE *REALLY* SORRY ABOUT

———

HUMAN BEINGS naturally feel remorseful when they've caused hurt or inconvenience or harm to another person. You bump into someone in a crowded subway car. You aim a soccer ball at the goal but instead it hits someone in the face. You're late with a report, which screws things up for your boss. You use harsh words to express your annoyance with someone and later get the feeling that you went too far. Something you did. Something you said. Something you failed to do or say. Disappointing another. Damaging property, either willfully or accidentally. Taking what's not yours. Breaking up with someone by text. Trespassing. Flaming, shaming, or outing someone on social media. Committing a traffic violation. Doing a substandard job. Ignoring social constraints.

What all these lapses and screw-ups have in common is that they are minor enough to mostly get away with. So the question of whether to fix the situation, to make it right through a formal, phased process of acknowledgment, restitution, and changed subsequent behavior, falls squarely on you.

But it's not always easy to do this right. There must be hundred ways to make a bad apology. So let's review a few guidelines for a good one.

Apology do's and don'ts

DON'T

Don't dilute the apology with an excuse. "I know I shouldn't have spent my year-end bonus on a big blow-out party with the guys when we've been saving for a new couch, but you should really let me have a little freedom now and then. I'm really starting to feel stifled in this relationship."

Don't try to cover up what you did. "I know it's wrong, but I won't get caught." You procrastinate on a report your boss has asked for, and then rush to get it done by borrowing figures from another report. Of course, you can't admit it to your boss, so you cover it up. Now you're constantly looking over your shoulder, wondering if you're ever going to get caught. You almost want to get caught. Suddenly you hate the job you used to love.

Don't compound the problem by putting off the apology. "I waited so long, now I can't apologize, even though it's eating away at me." You blow off something important, a friend's engagement party, or your dad's sixtieth birthday. Only later do you find out that not only were you missed, your thoughtlessness has also hurt someone you love. You know you should apologize, but the longer you wait, the worse it gets and the harder it is to reset the stage. Strike while the uh-oh feeling is strongest. Muster your courage, and get the job done.

Don't make excuses for dodging an apology you owe. "They know how I feel. I shouldn't have to say it." For reasons you can't really explain, you hate to apologize. It might be for any of the reasons already discussed in the earlier chapters of this book. Either way, you supplement your non-apology strategy with other methods, like over-explaining, ignoring them, or even being kind of a bully. If all else fails, you use passive aggression, making them feel like they owe you. Or you hold them hostage, threatening to leave the relationship (or the job or the apartment lease) if you don't get your way.

Don't reverse blame. "I'm sorry you got upset about what I did." As if their upset, and not your offending behavior, is the real problem.

Don't confuse getting caught with the offense itself. "This never would have come up if you hadn't looked at my phone." Getting caught might just be the angels of your better nature dragging you toward right behavior.

Don't go on and on about how bad you feel. "I don't know why I do these things. I'm a terrible person." This is not about you, it's about standing up and taking responsibility. Groveling and self-shaming makes them feel that they have to take care of you, as if you are the victim.

Don't argue or contradict them. "Okay, but it wasn't a Tuesday, it was a Wednesday." In the intensity of the moment, if something they've said is flat out wrong or inaccurate, just let it go. If it's crucial, at least ask for permission to clarify. Don't just jump in and tell them they're wrong, unless you want a whole new argument, new offenses, and a new apology on your to-do list.

Don't pretend everyone's cool without an apology. "Hey, are you still not talking to me?" No one buys it. And you've just committed another offense.

DO

Learn to recognize when you've hurt someone, even unconsciously or accidentally. Look for the signs in their emotions, what they say, or the uh-oh feeling in your tummy.

As soon as you can, plan and execute your four-step apology. Make a date to meet face to face.

Look the other person in the eyes as you speak. It shows you're sincere about making things right, inspires trust, and infuses you with courage.

Speak your piece, then shut up and let them speak theirs. Giving them a chance to respond promotes faster healing.

Remember that this is about them, not you. Worry less about your own comfort and preferences and more about your original intention to make things right with this person.

Learn to listen without interrupting. It builds character.

Keep your promises. Whether it's paying for damage, doing more of the housework, or showing up on time, be as good as your word.

TABLE OF APOLOGIES

	Small	Medium	Large	Big Gulp
Friends or roommates	Being rude, inconsiderate, or offensive	Taking the best seat, closet, or slice of pizza; never picking up the tab	Doing costly damage, e.g., getting drunk and puking on their furniture	Doing harm that involves the law, e.g., crashing their car or defaulting on a lease
Suggested apology	Sorry, man, that was rude.	I've been pretty inconsiderate lately. Hey, this one's on me.	I'm so sorry. It won't happen again. Please let me pay for the cleaning.	I really let you down. I'm trying to be a better person. Tell me how much I owe you and how I can make it up to you.
Lover or partner	Being lazy, messy, inattentive, or late	Embarrassing or disrespecting them in front of family or friends; teasing, bullying, or ghosting	Lying about condom use, birth control, sexual health; any lie to weasel out of responsibility	Betraying a trust or having an affair
Suggested apology	I'm sorry. I know I say that over and over, but I'll try to do better.	I don't know what came over me. I treated you horribly and I'm sorry. I won't do it again.	I should have told you the truth. How can I make it up to you?	You didn't deserve the way I treated you. Please forgive me. Can we work this out?

(continued)

	Small	**Medium**	**Large**	**Big Gulp**
Family member	Neglecting or forgetting birthdays or important occasions; never offering to help; only calling to ask for money	Failing to repay money you owe, gossiping or criticizing, or dredging up the past.	Not showing up for an important event like a wedding or a funeral	Physical violence or violating an order of protection
Suggested apology	I just called to see how you're doing. What's new and good?	Sorry. I've been a jerk. I'll try to do better. Tell me what I owe you.	I'm so sorry. I was selfish and inconsiderate, and I ruined it for you. Can you forgive me?	I'm sorry. I know that an apology doesn't change things or make up for what I did. I'm getting help.
Coworker	Failing to return calls or emails; arriving late or leaving early	Taking stuff from someone else's desk, the refrigerator, or the supply closet	Costing someone their job or throwing them under the bus	Bullying, intimidating, or sexually harassing
Suggested apology	Sorry. I'm being inconsiderate. I'll make it a point to do better.	Sorry, my mistake. I'm replacing the stuff I took.	I'm sorry I caused you this trouble. I shouldn't have said what I said. Can I go to your boss and explain?	Stop the behavior before the law comes after you. Get help if necessary, then leave them alone.

	Small	**Medium**	**Large**	**Big Gulp**
Boss	Missing a deadline	Submitting a report with errors in it	Receiving a critique about your work, and doing nothing to improve	Going over their head for your gain and their loss
Suggested apology	This was on me. I apologize. It won't happen again.	This was on me. I apologize. Let me rewrite the report.	I haven't been the best employee, but I appreciate your feedback. I'll work on improving.	I'm sorry for putting you in a tough position. I should have talked to you first. How can I make this right?
Stranger or random encounter	Arriving late to a theater performance and stepping on toes as you take your seat	Spilling something hot or messy on someone's clothing	Verbally harassing them or having a pointless confrontation	Physical violence
Suggested apology	I'm terribly sorry, please excuse me.	Oh, no! I'm so sorry! Let me help you with that.	I'm sorry that I got so heated. You may be right.	Back off. Shut up. Do whatever the police officers and lawyers tell you to do, and get help.

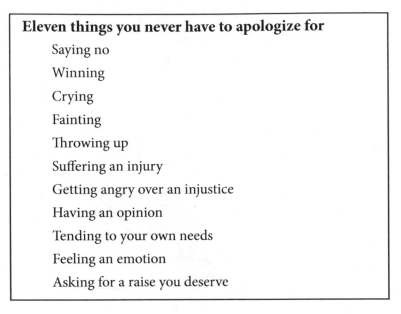

Eleven things you never have to apologize for

Saying no

Winning

Crying

Fainting

Throwing up

Suffering an injury

Getting angry over an injustice

Having an opinion

Tending to your own needs

Feeling an emotion

Asking for a raise you deserve

PART THREE

MASTERING THE
GOOD APOLOGY

———

CHAPTER 11
THE NINTH STEP OF ALCOHOLICS ANONYMOUS

———

IN REHABILITATION CLINICS, church basements, and shabby meeting rooms all over the world, people come together daily to do the work of recovering from addiction. The successful ones know recovery is not just about abstaining from the addictive substance or behavior but about changing from the inside. Alcoholics, drug addicts, bulimics, sex addicts, codependents, chronic gamblers, and compulsive people of every stripe—that is, the ones who want to recover—know that defeating the demons that once drove their destructive behavior requires a vigorous effort to mend their ways.

Being a better person is hard work and a lifetime job. It's why people who've gone years without a drink or a drug keep going to those meetings. It's why, on the wall of every meeting room of every twelve-step recovery program, you'll see a list of instructions for freeing oneself of the impulses and behaviors that bedevil the heart of every addict. As codes of living go, these twelve steps are not a bad way to straighten up and fly right, whatever your level of crookedness.

For our purposes, we'll be looking at step nine, which is making amends to those we've harmed. I asked a guy, sober for eight years in Alcoholics Anonymous (AA), to tell us everything he knows about the practice. Let's call him "Rafe." Of course, that's not his real name. Every practitioner of every form of public media is morally and ethically bound to keep secret the identity of every member of AA.

Alcoholics in recovery spend a lot of time looking at the mess they've made. They've got that uh-oh feeling down to a science, and they know that admitting their mistakes is only the beginning of the cleanup. The question is, what are you going to do about it? The answer is to make amends to those they have harmed.

Rafe explains that he and the guys he sponsors always start by taking an honest look at the harm they've done and resolving to make it right. They have made a list of all the people they've screwed over, and their job is to make amends to all of them. Even if the list contains twenty people, they go through the list, one at a time, until they're all done. They are virtuosos of moral integrity.

Here's more from Rafe. "I have the guy track down every person on his list and prepare an individualized approach to each one." If they can't find the right words to start, Rafe gives them a script that goes something like this: "I know I've caused you pain (or inconvenience, or frustration, or havoc) through my actions, and I want to make it right."

The benefit of prep work for this kind of apology is that it's more than just tossing off a quick "I'm sorry." It requires sinking down into the other person's experience and truly understanding what the apology is for. The object of this first approach is setting a date to meet with the person and *then* delivering the apology. In AA and elsewhere, the face-to-face apology is the best way to go. It's best not to try and wing it in a chance encounter or, God forbid, in a voicemail or text message. But sometimes you have no choice.

Sometimes when you first make contact, the other person might be wary. They very likely resent you, probably don't trust you, and may even be predisposed to hate you for the very offense you're hoping to clear up. Just in case they don't get past the door, Rafe prepares the guys he mentors to deliver the apology on the spot, if necessary. It's one of the few situations where it's acceptable to make your amends over the phone.

Right from the beginning, he tells them, let the other person call the shots. It may be humbling, but the whole point of the exercise is to fix what you broke or ruined. So you treat them with the utmost courtesy, being as obliging as possible without becoming a doormat.

Once you've made a date, you show up at the agreed upon place, on time and with your head held high. Even though you may feel awkward and uncomfortable, the result will be worth it. "Be brave," Rafe tells them. "You got this."

In the moment of awkward silence with the offended individual, you restate your mission. Say what you did in one sentence if you can. This helps you avoid graphic details that might sink the whole enterprise. Plainly state the harm you caused them ("I never paid back that money, even though back then I knew you were barely making rent.") Say the words "I'm sorry." You can add "It won't happen again," or "I'm really trying to be a better person," as long as it's genuine. Whatever you do, don't defend your actions. A true amends has no "but."

Then, he says, let the conversation go wherever it needs to go. The other person may be quiet as they take in what you've said. Then again, they may launch into a tirade. Chances are, if they've agreed to meet with you, they probably need it as much as you do. So, after you state your case, wait and see what happens.

While you may not have a monkey on your back driving you to do this step, it's worth it to consider this advanced-level amends. If you're avoiding someone, losing sleep, or tormented by something you did, you have nothing to lose by trying this four-step process. Take a page from Rafe and the men he mentors and go for it. And prepare to be amazed.

Brutal honesty smackdown

Years ago at my church, I was asked to join a small committee to evaluate the performance of an intern minister. The process involved completing a comprehensive set of questions that addressed the intern's skill in areas like preaching, pastoral visits, working with the children and youth, appearance, and communication skills. On every page was a reminder to be kind yet candid. Our honest feedback, the note assured us, was the only way these young divinity students could grow into the minister they hoped to be.

On the appointed day, the committee gathered with the pastor and the intern, a woman in her mid-thirties who had left a career as a first-grade teacher to pursue the ministry. Each member of the committee was instructed to deliver the key points of the evaluations directly to her. The pastor was present to maintain an appropriately safe and compassionate space while difficult truths were addressed.

My evaluation of the young intern was largely positive, but she had a few odd mannerisms, and she dressed like a throwback from the 1960s. Those Birkenstocks and flowy maxi dresses just got on my nerves.

My turn at feedback came, and I wondered how to phrase my thoughts in a compassionate but helpful way. The best I could come up with was, "Carina, your appearance is somewhat casual and even girlish. I recommend you consider getting some help with your wardrobe."

There was an awkward lull in the conversation, and suddenly Carina burst into tears. I felt a stab of regret. Through her tears she managed to say that my remarks had struck deep into her past when all her clothes came from Goodwill while her family lived on the meager wages her parents earned in blue collar jobs. She admitted to a lifelong struggle with the secret belief that her clothes were not good enough, and getting dressed every day was fraught with anxiety.

While I sank into my chair with shame and guilt, Carina had the grace to thank me for my feedback, an utterly selfless gesture that still makes me cringe with remorse. The evaluation session continued, but I was in another world. I felt terrible. I was filled with remorse for having unwittingly hurt this innocent person with my misbegotten feedback. I had meant to be helpful, but it had come out all wrong. I wrestled with my conscience for a few days, losing sleep as I struggled to find a way to make things right. I knew I couldn't bear the thought of seeing Carina at church the following Sunday without fixing the mess I'd made. I invited her to join me for tea at a café near our church, and I made my amends, which went something like this:

"Carina, I hurt you terribly with my judgments about your appearance. I won't hide behind my good intentions to give an honest critique, because I obviously judged you unfairly. Your story about your childhood opened my eyes. I'm sorry that I didn't try to learn more about you before I tried to evaluate your performance. I hope you can forgive me."

Our visit lasted two hours, in which Carina told me more about her childhood, her intentions for her future ministry, and her efforts to get some help with her appearance. It turned out her wild hair and Birkenstocks were an issue for others as well. It was painful, but it was also healing. During the remaining months of Carina's internship, we were friendly, even closer because of what had transpired.

Sealing the deal

Your next task in making an apology is to ask what it would take for the debt to be squared. Then shut up and listen. You might be tempted to promise that it won't happen again. If you do, you'd better mean it. You can't promise perfection, but you can at least try to change.

You'll be amazed at what people will say to you in the moments that follow an apology. Recall that few will ever experience such a moment in their lifetime. Someone who has been holding them hostage with heartache, resentment, or betrayal has come to set them free. For most people on the receiving end of a good apology, the response is true connectedness, a moment in which they sincerely find it in their heart to forgive you, or at least try. When you go to such lengths to try and change, people usually meet you halfway.

Occasionally you'll get someone who decides to be a jerk about it. "Yeah, you've owed me that money for ten years and *now* you want to pay it back? What about all the interest it might have earned?" There's a way to handle that, which we'll get into in Chapter 12. And what if the person tells you to take your apology and shove it? Easy. You just thank them for their time and leave. What they think of you is none of your business. You've told the truth and cleaned the slate. You went high when they went low. You've earned the right to be free of any guilt, remorse, or shame that you might have had lingering around. Enjoy the feeling of a clear conscience.

Still, you should be prepared for a few awkward moments. The object of your apology (and your harm) may have harbored their own resentments against you. They might still hate your damn guts, and they especially don't enjoy sitting only a few feet away from them, asking for forgiveness. Some people will want to end the conversation as quickly as possible. Fathers have a habit of doing this. This is way too much emotion for a lot of twentieth-century dads.

Your person might even be a little dismissive, airily brushing off the offense as if they had never even noticed it. Mothers have a way of doing this. They'll say, "Oh that was nothing. I'm your mother, and I love you. Don't even mention it." Know what you should do? Don't even mention it. Remember Rafe's advice: let them take the lead in the conversation. You're there to make things right with them, not control the outcome.

Occasionally you will apologize for something that has been tormenting you, yet the other person barely remembers it. You may have avoided them for years because of your own guilt—just one more reason why this exercise is so freeing. Now that your relationship is repaired, you can drop the rock and start fresh.

The most common reaction is that people are deeply moved by a formal amends. Their heart may be opening, right before your eyes. They listen very intently, and may well up or cry. It's an amazing feeling when someone you care about finally acknowledges a deep hurt. They are relieved, amazed, and gratified by the reconciliation they thought would never come.

Signal before changing lanes

If you're tempted to bask a while in this tender moment, just beware of either belaboring the offense or dashing off too soon. With a fragile new connection just being forged, and the sweetness of reconciliation infusing the scene, some are tempted to spill all the beans of their past transgressions. When admitting you haven't been a good son, it is unwise to recount every time you took money out of your mom's wallet or failed to flush the toilet, or to blithely announce to a co-worker, "I'm sorry I've hated you all these years."

The key is to remember that you've come to them to make things right, not unburden your conscience. This is not to say that telling all is never a good idea. In fact the moment may call for it. You'll be talking about the time you held your brother in a hammerlock until he wet himself, and suddenly another, much more egregious offense will spring to mind. Apologize for that, too. Winging it is okay in this instance. Or the person themselves may bring up another injury or insult, one that you were unaware of or had forgotten.

So before you go, be sure to ask the important question, "Did I leave anything out?"

When a couple I know did this exercise, the husband finished his spiel, looked at his wife with an expectant smile and asked, "Did I leave anything out?" Whereupon she started ticking off a list of his hurts and offenses.. She mentioned at least a dozen slights and screw-ups that he'd either completely forgotten, dismissed as unimportant, or rationalized, falling victim to the fundamental attribution error.

This is actually a good thing. If someone accepts your invitation to speak up about a past injury, it means they are fully engaged in what you're trying to do. They want things to be better, too. You've connected in a way that wasn't safe to do before. But now you've proven yourself trustworthy, ethical, and courageous. By facing your own faults head on, you've laid them out like so many weapons the other person could easily use against you.

Vulnerable? Hell, yeah. But vulnerability is what makes this exercise so powerful. You've entered a plea of guilty and thrown yourself on the mercy of the Court of Them. It's incredibly humbling and even a little scary, but it's also freeing. When the individual who is the object of your apology recognizes your profound act of humility and faith, they usually respond with their own ethical, gracious, human response. They forgive you.

Very little in life is quite as exhilarating and liberating as a good apology. It's like paying off an emotional debt. You've repaid the other person for all the heartache they've suffered at your hands. Sitting there across from the other person, fences mended, defenses dropped, trust restored, most people are overcome with a sense of great peace and release. The upset is gone, the wound has started to heal. You both feel relieved and probably happier. In most cases you'll find your relationship is closer than ever. A lot of good can come out of an amends delivered in this way.

But there can be other reactions, too, so let's talk about some of them. Sometimes the person has been so deeply wounded that they can't get their head around what you're doing. The reaction is, essentially, "Not good enough. I don't forgive you. Get out." If this happens to you, the first thing to do is stay calm. Remember all the reasons why you are apologizing, that is, to make things right on your end. Your role is not to manage or control the other person's emotions, or to make your own life easier. So, let them rant. Resist the temptation to defend yourself. You might try repeating, "I know I've messed up. You're right to be pissed." Then you might add, "Is there anything I can do to make things right?"

If this keeps on, or starts going in circles, then it's time to go. If you can still get a word in edgewise, tell them you hope you can make it up to them someday, and you understand if they're just not ready. Thank them for taking the time to listen to you. Then say goodbye and leave immediately.

Do *not* try to engage them. The quickest way to escalate someone else's anger is to meet it with your own. If a person is still red-faced and furious, it's best to step away. But do it kindly, not with more anger. It may take all the self-control you have, but you'll only have more to regret and apologize for if you cave in to your emotions at this delicate stage.

There can be dozens of reasons why the other person just can't deal with your apology, some of which may have little to do with you. They might be genuinely freaked out when they realize that you are vulnerable, that they are in control and could even hurt you if they wanted to. That's too much for some people, and it can kick up all kinds of deep stuff that you shouldn't try to handle. You did what you came to do. Wish them well and make your exit.

The second kind of unexpected response is that the person needs something more. You can detect this by the way they're behaving. If they still can't meet your eyes, won't stop fidgeting, or their face is like stone, there's probably something going on. If you haven't done so already, it's time to ask, "Is there anything else I can do to make this right?" Sometimes people need a tangible expression of your remorse and your intention to change. A lot of things come into play. Remember you're there to mend what's broken, so stay in the moment until they've had a chance to answer..

Now that you've done everything you can to right a wrong, a door has closed behind you. Like Jason Lee in "My Name is Earl," you can take a certain pleasure in crossing another name off your list. Enjoy the sense of relief, the lighter step, the clear conscience. You might even find it a little easier to look people in the eye. You're a little less weighed down by people and situations that might have once seemed impossible to fix. You've proven you can be courageous and upstanding. You've faced down your demons and your fears and emerged victorious.

CHAPTER 12
NO EXCUSES

———

ONCE YOU HAVE a little more practice at using this skill, you have a few tools in your back pocket that you can use to fix what's broken or damaged in your most important relationships. Strategize before leaping into the fray.

Sometimes an apology should be accompanied by restitution. In the monetary sense, this is obvious. If you cracked up someone's car, of course you will have already offered to pay for the repair, the increased insurance, and any other harm that may have come to them or others because of your mistake. But restitution also means fixing what you damaged, paying back what you borrowed, taking down the offending post, or even apologizing to a third party. "Brianna, I'm sorry I kept Matt out barhopping until 4 a.m. the night before your wedding."

In many cases, as with other formal amends we've covered, the person on the receiving end of your apology may let you off the hook. But don't presume. When you owe someone a big chunk of money, or when you owe lots of people a big chunk of money, the thing to do is to face it squarely. Explain to the lender that you want to make good on your debt. If you're not exactly flush, ask if you can pay it back in small installments. You'd be surprised how many people will let you pay back as little as $25 a month if they know you're sincere and you're good for it. Even banks and businesses to which you owe money will sometimes forgive debts, or at least make it easy to pay them back. Paying your debts is an amazing feeling while you're doing it, and feels almost miraculous when you've paid it down to zero. If you're carrying debt or student loans, and you've just been falling behind, work it out. Start paying it off. You're a new person now. The old behavior will not stand.

CASE STUDY

Sophie spent most of her twenties ingesting small mountains of cocaine. She managed to land a job at a pharmacy, which was owned and operated by a pharmacist we'll call Dr. Hemingway. Her problem reached a peak shortly after she was hired, primarily due to Sophie's habit of liberally sampling the merchandise. During the few months she worked there, she managed to steal something on the order of $10,000 worth of cocaine from the back room of the pharmacy.

The rest of Sophie's story of decline and dissolution is long and ugly, but eventually she turned a corner. She fought hard to get clean and build a new drug-free life for herself. But along the way, Sophie's sponsor insisted she would never truly recover and might even use again if her crime, which miraculously had gone undetected, continued to weigh on her spirit. Sophie's sponsor insisted she needed to make a formal amends for what she had done. That mean not only going to Dr. Hemingway and confessing her wrongdoing, but also making restitution for the cost of the drugs she had stolen.

The whole prospect of this enterprise terrified Sophie. Even if Dr. Hemingway didn't report her to the police, she knew that she could never pay back this debt if she gave him every paycheck until the day she died. She dreaded making amends, but the guilt was ruining her health. But Sophie was straightening up every other aspect of her life, and she couldn't let this hang out there, haunting her forever. She resolved to take the leap and own her actions, come what may.

Sophie tracked down Dr. Hemingway, and learned that he had retired, and the pharmacy where she had once worked was no more. Of course, this didn't let her off the hook, so she pressed on, locating an email address and sending him a message that went something like this: "Dr. Hemingway, I'm not sure if you remember me, but I worked for you for a few months in 2006. I had a terrible drug problem back then, and I did some things I regretted. I'm hoping you'll meet with me so that we can talk about it."

Sophie wisely avoided incriminating herself in writing, although her unspoken message would not be lost on the good doctor. For a week she waited for his reply, tormented by bad dreams of prison time. She was prepared to deal with whatever consequences there might be, including arrest, although a lawyer friend of hers, who agreed to back her up if necessary, believed this wouldn't be the case. "I kept asking myself, how free do I want to be?" Sophie recalls. A lifetime of sleepless nights was not part of her plan.

At last she heard from Dr. Hemingway. "I appreciate what you are attempting with your request to meet with me," he wrote back. "And I know full well what you did; in fact I knew about it while it was going on." That shocked her. "I'm grateful you've received the help you so desperately needed. Let's call this matter squared away. Good luck to you. Sincerely, W.F. Hemingway, D.Pharm."

Last known address

Say you had a falling out with a college roommate over money you owe them. Your newly awakened conscience won't let you ride on your former excuses, like "he deserved it," or "he owes me that money as payment for my time and trouble." But when you do track him down, you learn that he's moved to the Australian outback, and you have no idea how to reach him. What do you do?

First, beware of using it as an excuse to delay or avoid making the amends. Once we grow a conscience, it's a slippery slope when we start falling back into our old ways. They're much harder to correct the second time around. But if you've really tried your best to track the person down through social media channels, asking people you both know, or even by trying to locate the number you once scribbled in an old textbook, it's time to consider a few alternatives.

Letters are a highly underrated tool for getting your thoughts in order and communicating them to another person. Different from a post, tweet, or snap, it allows you to slow down and formulate your thoughts to a single person, not a feed or a group. It also gives you time to think of the best way to phrase your message. And if you physically mail your letter, you have the added benefit of sitting in not-knowingness for a while. Very Zen.

When a phone call is not possible (say you can't locate them because they've gone to live in a yurt on Mount Everest), a letter is not only practical and expedient, but it also offers many of the same advantages of a face-to-face meeting. Even better, because the person in your mind does not tap their foot or glare at you as you speak, you have the luxury of really getting it all out.

Do your best to prepare for your letter the same way you would if you were meeting in person. Your letter should focus only on what you did, not what they did. Let them know you understand that your actions hurt them, which you never meant to do, that it's not the kind of person you want to be, and that you hope to do better from now on. Choose words you would say to them if they were sitting in front of you. Remember the four steps, but also use the opportunity to go a little deeper. The insight will benefit you, making up for the possibility you may never say it in person.

1. Admit to the harm you caused to their well-being, sanity, or relationship with you.

2. Express remorse or regret for the mistakes you've made and the harm it's caused them, avoiding any criticism or pointing out what they might have contributed to the situation.

3. Fix it. Ask if there is anything they would like to add, and what you can do to make it up to them.

4. Change your behavior. Keep your promises.

The key is to access the same frame of mind you had when you made up your mind to mend fences with this person. Think of the letter as the script you'd use if you were making the apology face to face.

Don't skip the part where you ask if they have anything to say. Ask that question of the universe and then listen. Your next move is to pay attention to what the universe does next. Sometimes fate has a funny way of acting in your best interests.

CASE STUDY

Tessa lived for about a year with Judy, a woman that she just didn't like. During the time they roomed together they socialized occasionally, but Tessa found they had little in common. When she and Judy eventually parted ways, Tessa felt relieved of the burden of trying to be friendly to someone she didn't regard as a friend.

Not so with Judy. Every couple of months or so, Judy would call to invite Tessa to go shopping, grab a coffee, see a movie, either with the hubbies or without. Tessa went along a few times, but the experiences only reinforced her conviction that she and Judy were a poor match as friends. She started to politely decline Judy's invites, which only made Judy more persistent. Finally Tessa had enough, and she resolved to tell Judy the truth.

She invited Judy out for coffee, and valiantly started off with an apology, even though up to now she had done no more harm than a bit of social lying. Tessa said, as kindly as she could manage, "I'm sorry if it seems like I'm dodging you, but I have to tell the truth. I think we just don't have that much in common. I appreciate your efforts to get together, but I'd really prefer that we go our separate ways." Tessa thought she was being considerate and honest, and she hoped, somewhat naively, that Judy might be relieved to hear the truth.

Most decidedly, that was not the case. Judy was hurt and angry, and the coffee date ended with Judy yelling at her, dissolving into tears, and storming out in a dreadful breakup drama. Tessa agonized over the incident. She knew she had really screwed it up but honestly had no idea how she could have handled it differently. Keep on faking it? Why was telling the truth not the answer? For months she wondered if she should call Judy to offer another apology, but worried it would look like she wanted to be friends. Guiltily, she accepted the rift as her salvation.

A couple of years went by. Tessa heard through mutual friends that Judy had divorced, remarried, and moved to another city. Time softened Tessa's opinion of Judy, and she realized that, even though she'd spoken the truth, and even though she wasn't prepared to reinstate their relationship, she was genuinely sorry she had hurt Judy's feelings. Tessa dutifully wrote out her four-step amends on an index card and stuck it in a deep pocket of her purse. She promised herself that if she and Judy ever crossed paths again, she was fully prepared to make the apology.

One sultry afternoon in July, Tessa was visiting the home of Ariel, a good friend from college who also knew Judy. They were sitting in the breezy kitchen of Ariel's beach rental, drinking iced tea and talking over old times as Ariel prepared dinner, when the house phone rang. Ariel's hands were busy, so Tessa picked up the receiver. It was Judy.

All she could think was, *What are the chances?*

For a minute, Tessa froze. Part of her wanted to disguise her voice and hand the phone over to Ariel, but the charade would only compound her guilt with a self-serving lie. Recalling the index card buried in the bottom of her purse, Tessa knew what she needed to say to make things right with Judy. Tessa identified herself to the surprised woman on the other end of the line. She began by offering an apology for not being a good friend, acknowledging the hurt she'd caused by ignoring Judy's attempts to remain close. She finished with, "I'm really sorry for the things I said that hurt you. Anytime you want to get together for lunch or a cup of coffee, I'd be really happy to see you." This last part was unplanned, but suddenly she felt unburdened, and it changed her entire outlook. She found herself accepting Judy's friendship, since apparently that was her fate. The offer to get together was sincere.

On the other end of the phone, Judy went silent as stone. Tessa asked, "Is there anything you'd like to say to me about all this?" After another silence, Judy said quietly, "Thank you for the apology. I think you were right when you said we just don't have much in common. Now, would you give the phone to Ariel? I need to talk to her." Ouch. That stung a little, even if Tessa probably deserved it. Tessa realized that her work was done. Her rift with Judy had been successfully repaired, although not the way she had expected. She no longer had to feel guilty or worry about running into Judy. She was free.

Taking your apology to the grave

What if you need to make amends to someone who has died?

You might think you're off the hook, but as those who've been haunted by the ghosts of their own crimes and misdemeanors can tell you, it takes a lot of energy to stuff down the guilt of hurtful behavior that has literally gone to the grave without apology. Unless you're okay with carrying that weight for the rest of your life, you'll need to find another way to make it up to them.

Introducing the graveside apology.

Approach it the same way you would with someone you haven't been able to track down: write a letter. The same elements of Tessa's "maybe someday" index card apply here, too.

Follow the four-step process. Admit to the harm you caused them. Apologize and say you want to set things right. Express your regret. Declare your intention to do better.

Now go to the cemetery and read it at their grave.

Okay, that's a big ask. But few gestures are as powerful or freeing as a graveside apology. Just know you'll feel like an idiot, especially if there are other people around, so try to plan accordingly. One strategy is to read your letter silently or in a whisper.

Then pause to listen. You only need a minute or two. Listen for a thought or phrase that may come into your mind. It may be something like, "It's okay. I forgive you." Or, "It doesn't matter anymore. Move on." Or, "Be quicker next time." It's your intuition, the only communication device the universe has. Consider it your answer and your absolution.

A small personal ritual can make your graveside apology more meaningful and powerful. Take your cue from other cemetery traditions, like placing pebbles on the headstone, lighting a candle, or planting flowers. All good. Don't forget, it's more for you than for them.

If the deceased is currently resting in an urn on someone's mantelpiece, you'll need to devise another setting for your apology ritual. You might choose a place you both loved to go, perhaps bringing an item that reminds you of your time together. Music helps, too. Choose a song that helps your heart open, or with lyrics that deftly sum up your feelings toward them. Light your candle, fire up the player on your phone, sit in silence for a few minutes. When you feel the time is right, deliver your apology. You can read it or wing it. When you're finished, ask your question, "Is there anything I've left out that you want to mention?" And wait for a response.

You may "hear" something you weren't expecting or that doesn't seem to make sense. An image of them might come to mind, or you'll recall one of their quirks, or you'll flash on a conversation you once had with them. You might experience something entirely different, like a dream.

My friend Jade owed an apology to her mother, who had passed away. As a child and throughout her teens, Jade had always gone to her mother for advice, but as Jade got older, they had drifted away from the practice. Her mother had died suddenly after a brief illness, and there hadn't been time to repair the relationship. Jade carried the burden for years, telling herself there was nothing she could do, until she tried the graveside apology. In the silence that followed her reading of the letter, Jade suddenly had a vivid waking dream. She imagined she was getting her hair cut, and when she got up from the chair, Jade noticed the stylist had left a long hank of hair dangling down her back.

She sensed immediately that it was a message from her mother about Jade's current boyfriend. The guy was lazy, selfish, and clueless about how to be in a relationship, but Jade kept hoping she could somehow reform him. Her dream brought these flaws into sharp focus. "I mean, what kind of hairdresser misses something as obvious as a long hank of hair? The kind you need to get rid of."

Jade dumped her boyfriend that afternoon. In the months following the graveside apology that led to her vision, Jade has "talked" to her mom regularly, asking for advice and often receiving answers in the form of compelling images or wise words. She swears they're just like the ones her mother would have offered as comfort and counsel when Jade was young.

After trying it once, you can repeat a ritual or create a new one any time you feel the urge. People often find a new sense of connection and completion with someone important to them who had passed on, a bond they'd assumed was broken forever.

Not so fast

If you've set your mind to cleaning the slate, there's no reason to weasel out of making things right with everyone you harmed, including someone who is better off never seeing your sorry face again. The list includes former mistreated lovers who have moved on, classmates or fellow campers you bullied, drug dealers you cheated, and married people with whom you dallied.

In each of these cases you'd likely do more harm by stirring up the past than you did through the original offense. Even the most egregious sins can be made worse if you show up out of the past and reopen old wounds with someone who has been trying to put it all behind them. I'm not saying it's never appropriate to track someone down for a sincere apology, but if your goal is merely to let yourself off the hook, think about what it would do to them. If your shadow on their doorstep would cause more pain, don't do it.

Find a charitable organization that rectifies the kind of harm you did and become a volunteer or a regular donor. Your steady efforts to put goodness back into the world in the place where you took some away will close the loop and mend your heart.

CHAPTER 13
BANISHING DEMONS

———

THE FRAMEWORK FOR the graveside apology works whether a relationship has been reasonably good and loving or just kind of meh. But not every apology goes out to someone you loved. In this chapter we'll deal with bad people, sick people, criminals, lawyers and doctors who hide their mistakes, and true scoundrels who seem bent on doing you wrong. Sometimes apologizing is a really terrible idea. Admitting your guilt to the victim of your error, much less apologizing for it, is at best ill advised, and at worst, dangerous. No, I'm not talking about the difficulty of apologizing to someone who intimidates you, or when your offense is shameful, or when the consequences of your behavior lands you in hot water, like repaying a massive debt, incurring criminal charges, or even losing your job. I'm talking about the dangers of dealing with people who are not stable enough to be trusted with the truth. Such people are sick, and they will react to your honesty and vulnerability, not with forgiveness or relief, but with a twisted desire to retaliate. You need to be smart about this, so let's regroup for a second.

Addiction, mental illness, crime, and violence can pose almost insurmountable barriers to a sincere attempt to make things right. Learn to distinguish between what you have contributed to a bad situation and the wrongs perpetrated by others. Sometimes admitting your part, if only to yourself or a trusted confidante, can be just as freeing as apologizing. If the other person in this scenario is just so sick or caught up in something uncontrollable to the degree that they just aren't capable of reacting in a humane way, it's important to recognize when you should forge ahead with your apology and when you should just keep your mouth shut and avoid the person entirely.

Dangerous intersection ahead

You might be someone who was, if you'll pardon the expression, raised by wolves. I mean, people savagely incapable of looking out for anyone but themselves. People caught in a web of drugs, alcohol, or crime or plagued by mental illness. Such unfortunates are so spectacularly unsuited to raising children that laws should be passed against it.

My friend Maisie grew up in a household with an alcoholic father and a mother whose religious convictions prevented her from leaving her abusive husband. Every night when Maisie's father would come home from work, she and her two brothers would watch through the window. The manner in which their father pulled his car into the driveway predicted the kind of night they could expect. If he emerged from the car with a jaunty expression, or if he was carrying gifts or flowers for their mother, Maisie knew they were safe, and they might even have a rare evening of family fun. But, if the car screeched to a halt in the driveway and the slam of the car door shook the front windows, Maisie and her brothers would hide in their rooms.

Maisie's father would never admit to being wrong. On bad nights, after he was finished screaming insults or kicking in doors or terrorizing their mother, he would eventually calm down. But for hours after these outbursts a traumatized Maisie would remain shivering in her room. One night, in a drunken rage, he stumbled over one of her favorite toys, a robot puppy named Rickles. Diving for the toy, she was too late. Maisie watched in horror as her father hurled it to the floor and stamped on the pieces. Crying, she ran to her room, leaving the dismembered Rickles where he'd fallen, and where her father discovered it the next day. Hungover and sullen, he growled, "Clean up that mess. And get over it. You're too old for toys."

You may know someone who grew up in this kind of household, or maybe awful stuff like this happened to you. You didn't deserve it, nor should you have to carry the weight of it for the rest of your life.

Here's a word of caution. What I'm about to say may upset some readers, so if you have the slightest concern about sparking a post-traumatic reaction from your own past, stop reading and check in with your support system. People who've grown up in a household like Maisie's often struggle to adapt to their parents' irrational behaviors, which can veer wildly between raging and abusive (sometimes involving sexual or emotional violence) or repentant and overcompensating. Most of these children defy the odds and grow up to be decent, sober, contributing members of society who have succeeded in breaking the cycle of abuse.

But, misshapen by the insanity in their household, some abuse victims become abusers themselves. They can display many of the same problems, from drug or alcohol addiction to emotional and mental instability to violence. Their behavior can sometimes be worse than what they witnessed or experienced as a child. Approaching such a person with an apology is not safe.

A corollary here might be difficult to accept, which is that being the victim of abuse doesn't automatically make a person innocent of all wrongdoing. You still need a way to clear off your side of the street so you can be free of any guilt, remorse, shame, or any of the other demons that may linger long after the abuse has ended.

Why subject yourself to this kind of painful scrutiny? You haven't forgotten the abuse, although you may have repressed the experience so that you can barely remember it, or can't remember it at all. Or you might harbor fantasies of murder or mayhem befalling your abuser as payback for the way they treated you. If the damage still has hooks in you, it is still affecting you, and you're not free.

Imagine this scenario: that when you were small and dependent on the adults in your life to protect and care for you, something horrendous happened, like a nasty uncle who fondled you, an alcoholic mother who wouldn't acknowledge you until she had her tumbler of vodka, or a father who gambled away the rent money so you and your mom had to live in a shelter for a while. You were not responsible in any way for the harms they visited on you.

Yet as an adult, you may be still harboring demons, believing that the abuse happened because of something you did wrong or something that was wrong *with you*. This all-too-common line of childish thinking can lead an abuse victim to nurture and protect a smoldering ember of anger, grief, hatred, or self-loathing. Instead of releasing it once the abuse has ended, they hold onto it, hiding it from the world like Gollum's Precious.

While most abuse survivors grow up to become wonderful people, they still may be harboring the abuse deep inside, where Gollum's ring continues to leach out poison. Regardless of whether a horrific childhood creates a tortured adult obeying their inner demons or one who can shed their terrible past to become a pillar of the community, they are still carrying around the poison inside, as if hoping it will eventually kill their abuser.

How free do I want to be?

Liberating yourself from the dead weight of an abuser in your head all your life needs to be done the right way. You'll want to tread carefully. It's vitally important to loop in someone who knows your story, for example, a therapist, close friend or sibling, or spouse or partner. Let them know what you're up to and why you're doing it. You shouldn't be trying this on your own. If you and your advisor agree you can handle it, the format is the same as for a graveside apology.

Maybe this is the right place to carefully examine the word "amends." Webster's defines the word "amend" as "improve, make better, remove the faults of, correct, or to change or revise or improve one's conduct." Making amends is putting things to rights.

I've heard it said that "amendment" means change, but the meaning is more subtle than insert, add, or delete. Let's use the U.S. Constitution for our example. An amendment cannot and does not change history. It can't remove or undo any of the words or practices that were set in place by the original Constitution, nor does it alter the fact that our country once condoned slavery or withheld voting rights from women. But it does change the living document in order to make things right.

Stemming from the root of the word meaning "to mend," the goal of making amends is to set things right going forward. When you've mended a broken table leg or a torn blouse or a lacerated tendon, the thing mended will never again be like new, but it can be functional, serviceable, even beautiful again, scars, nail holes, lumpy stitches, and all.

Amending the mistakes of a poorly made childhood works the same way. Your part in it was not that you "asked for it." Even having done something you shouldn't have done, something you believe might have set the abuser off, doesn't justify the abuse. That's not the part I'm talking about.

Ask yourself, how have I allowed the abuse to rule over everything I've tried to build in my life? Am I keeping it alive with resentment and bitterness? Do I ever tell the story for effect, even embellishing it for sympathy? Do I nurture and protect it like Gollum's ring? When you allow the resentment of an old wound to influence your attitude toward life, love, intimacy, relationship, parenting, and a host of other things in your life, you're keeping the infection alive. No one else is doing it to you, and no one but you is suffering the consequences.

If you have mistrusted everyone, judged too quickly, or even hidden your own light to avoid any inkling of a situation where you might be abused again, then you have been living your life with one foot on the accelerator and the other on the brake. If you're like most human beings, you've blamed it on other people. The abuser. The adults around you who couldn't or wouldn't protect you. The people who looked at you differently after they found out what happened to you, and who might have even judged, blamed, or shunned you. Most of all, you've probably blamed yourself.

That's one big maxed-out lie. If you've been living that lie, trying to carry on with the half-life you opted for after the abuse, that's what you need to amend.

Breaking chains

Start by thinking about who was harmed. Here again is where a letter can serve you well. Getting it all down in black and white can work wonders toward helping you gain perspective. It also gives you something to show to your trusted advisor, who can check it out and offer their thoughts.

We're operating from the assumption that, for all the reasons discussed, you're not going to deliver this in person. Think about how you want to go about the job of breaking the chain. Do you want to scream out your rage and pain, throw some dishes, or spend an hour at the gym working the heavy bag? Do you want to list all the torment and suffering abusive actions caused you and read it out loud to the abuser's photograph? You could try a technique some psychotherapists recommend: imagine the abuser is sitting in an empty chair and let fly with everything you've ever wanted to say to their face.

But here again is a cautionary note. Remember we're not psychologists dealing with the mind, we're human beings dealing with the spirit. Now is a good time to remind you that no book should be used as a substitute for psychotherapy. If you think you need professional help to deal with your past, be safe and smart and take yourself to a care provider.

The spiritual cleansing of old wounds begins with asking yourself, what would free my spirit from the clutches of my abuser? Although it can help to consider that they were probably sick, ignorant, or possibly a victim of abuse themselves, be mindful that creating a fantasy that allows you to forgive them can bring reality crashing down on you if you find out that it wasn't remotely true. Maybe they really *were* a malevolent force.

Another line of thinking is to accept that the past can't be changed, which is a hard truth to swallow. Your grief may come roaring to the surface, forcing you to drop everything and deal with your emotions for a while. Try to do this without help from indulging in food, behaviors, or mind-altering substances that take you out of yourself. The hurt will still be here when you get back. Try healthy outlets like spending time with pets, close friends, or even favorite blankies. All three are really good companions on this journey. So are therapists, so never dismiss that option.

If you've decided to write a letter, start by sketching out your apology script. It could go something like this.

"To whom it may concern: You did something to me that I haven't been able to forgive. Holding onto that anger and hatred and allowing it to excuse behavior of my own of which I'm not proud was my choice. I regret how I handled this, and I'm ready to change. I release you from my anger, grief, resentment, and fears."

Play around with the language. Show your trusted advisor and get their input. Make sure it really feels right to you.

Determine the time and place for your amends ritual. There's always the graveside, if applicable, or any other place that's private and safe—an open field under a sunny, cloudless sky, sitting on a boulder in the middle of a river, or in the woods next to a friendly campfire. Make it *your* ritual. Remember this is not about them. The sooner you stop making it about them, the more peace, energy, and free space you can reclaim for yourself.

Don't forget to ask the question, "Is there anything you'd like to say to me?" Then wait, and listen. If you get nothing but crickets, fine. They're just not talking. Maybe they really were a bad apple, so what did you expect?

As with other one-way apologies, sometimes you'll get a message.

The universe, God, Source, Higher Power, or whatever you call it, represents a connection to something intangible that speaks to us on the inside. It might come as a still small voice or a feeling without words. Maybe you will hear something like, "It's over." Or you might hear something instructional, like "Tell your brother about this," or a sudden insight like, "I hate that freaking job. I'm giving notice on Monday." Just bear in mind, the universe speaks in short sentences, so if what you hear sounds like a to-do list or a rant, it's not God. It's you. Pipe down and try again.

Either way, at the end of your ritual, pause. Take in a big deep breath of fresh air, wherever you may be. Congratulate yourself, and thank whatever it was that led you here. Because your side of the street is officially cleared off. You have nothing to hide, no evil Gollum's ring to harbor in your heart. You've broken the chains, and you're free.

CHAPTER 14
DO IT YOURSELF OR HIRE A PRO?

———

IN MOST SITUATIONS where a wrong must be made right, it's up to the person who recognizes it to make the first, and admittedly harder, move. But there are some situations where you shouldn't try to go it alone. There are other times when speaking up for yourself, and even demanding an apology or a change in behavior, accomplishes the same relief and healing that comes from doing it yourself. Let's start there.

The reverse amends

Maybe you yourself have been a victim. If you've suffered persistent mistreatment from another, ranging from disrespect to bullying to harassment, the solution is not to continue putting up with it. Sooner or later you have to speak up for yourself. Putting a stop to a bully or abuser's behavior—or at least calling them out—is another way of making things right.

Trey was ten when his parents divorced, and fourteen when his father remarried a woman who made zero effort to form a relationship with Trey or his two sisters. She had her man, and that was all she cared about.

Trey's stepmother, Mary Pat, was hypercritical of just about everyone. She picked on her husband, Trey and his sisters, neighbors, clerks, drivers, whether on the road or in the parking lot, and the people on television. She criticized everything and everyone like it was her job.

This behavior went on for years. Trey and his sisters put up with it because, as his older sister pointed out, "She makes Dad happy." But when the stepmother's criticisms began filtering down to Trey's own children and pets, he knew he had to speak up. At the family vacation home in Cape Cod, Mary Pat's criticism reached an intolerable level. Trey suggested sitting down for a heart-to-heart talk, but she kept putting him off. Trey decided to ambush her and waited until the next time she criticized someone. He didn't have long to wait.

Trey's ten-year-old son Declan had the audacity to use the wrong pan to scramble a batch of eggs. Upon entering the kitchen and surveying the scene, Grandma Mary Pat immediately laced into Declan, ridiculing him for his mistake, demanding to know whether his parents ever taught him a single thing, and refusing to let him clean the pan because he clearly didn't know his way around a kitchen. Declan fled, fighting back tears. Trey could take no more. Ablaze with paternal instinct and burning with pent up resentment, he told his stepmother, "In our family we don't talk to each other that way."

Mary Pat stopped in her tracks. Trey forged on, insisting that she immediately put a stop to her petty criticizing. He asked her to show more kindness toward his family and tolerance for any inadvertent mistakes the children might make. Then he delivered the zinger. "Just remember one thing—we've always treated you well because you're married to my father. But, if you refuse to change this behavior, you will no longer be welcome around my children."

It took time, but eventually Mary Pat changed her ways, and even though she never apologized, Trey felt the difference immediately. Clearly, she had been suffering from a big case of fundamental attribution error and had never once tried to put herself in someone else's shoes. Although she retained some of her prickly fastidiousness about the kitchen implements, and could not seem to stop herself from muttering at the television, she was more cordial when speaking to Trey, his kids, and even the dog.

Reporting someone to the authorities

Recognize when you have to step away from the spiritual toolkit and call the police. Say you've had a falling out with a brother-in-law, and he comes to your house with a baseball bat and starts smashing the headlights on your pickup. What should you do? Call the cops, of course! Do not attempt an apology, a five-and-five, or any other kind of coping tool that requires the cooperation of both parties. The guy is crazy, so unless you're a trained counselor or have some experience with intervention, don't try to fix this on your own.

Later—and depending on how things shake out with the brother-in-law—you might look at what part you played in his blind rage. An argument takes two people. In twelve-step programs an idea called the spiritual axiom exists, which is when I'm having a problem with you, something is going on with me too. Searching for your own mistakes can serve several important functions. At the very least, you owe your sister an honest assessment of what happened. Don't make the mistake of trashing her husband as a way of expressing solidarity. Tell her what happened without embellishment.

I'm not saying you have to take all the blame, but if you've learned anything from reading this far, you'll know it's likely you contributed something, even innocently or subconsciously, to your brother-in-law's rage. Maybe you borrowed something without asking or said something you shouldn't have said. You may have bragged about your successes, arousing jealousy or bitterness. Whatever your reasons for not liking him, instead of keeping it on the down low, maybe it's been coming out sideways. Malicious comments about him to your sister, subtle digs at his team preferences during a football game, or horseplay that ends with something getting mysteriously ripped or bloody are examples of these sideways expressions.

Check it out. Be honest. Going through the four steps to an apology will help you take responsibility for your part in the damage. Write it down first and share it with a close-mouthed friend for feedback. Then treat it like you would any amends, figuring out how to make your approach. Be smart because if matters have gotten really out of hand, for instance, if legal issues or problems beyond your scope have arisen, then stand down until you can see a way through it safely.

Is there a lawyer in the house?

Sometimes legal complications can prevent you from making an apology. Even a mild fender bender can cost you your shirt, simply because you stepped out of your car and immediately started apologizing. Being loose-lipped with "your part" can get you a summons and a big jump in your insurance premiums.

Other more serious issues, like a landlord or property dispute, contesting a will, challenging an illegal firing, appearing as a witness in court, accusing a coworker of sexual abuse, or whistleblowing on your company, require professional intervention. These situations are ripe for passing blame around like a bottle around a campfire. Use your Spidey sense to determine whether to make a course correction or formally apologize, then run it by a trusted advisor.

I'm not suggesting you sit by, saying nothing while someone goes away for years because your lawyer insisted you stick with her script for the case. You still need to follow your heart and listen to your conscience. If you feel a strong sense that you won't be able to live with yourself if you don't set things right, talk to your lawyer about it. If she's any good, she'll figure out a way through the minefield of self-incrimination so you don't end up with a life sentence of no sleep. (Did I mention that a clear conscience makes the softest pillow?)

In her excellent book, *The Art of the Apology: How, When, and Why to Give and Accept Apologies,* author Lauren M. Bloom, J.D., spells out the right way to deliver an effective apology when facing a lawsuit or malpractice suit. While this may not apply to you, her advice is helpful to consider. She begins with the basic premise that an apology is first and foremost an attempt to take responsibility for one's actions. She writes, "From your defense attorney's perspective, however, taking responsibility is essentially the same as admitting that you breached your duty of care."

Bloom goes on to enumerate the benefits of apologizing when the time is right, preferably before a lawsuit is filed and with the blessing of your attorney. "A well-timed and effective apology … can fend off the blame-and-shame cycle, and can even prevent a lawsuit from being filed in the first place."

Likewise, in the life-and-death arena of health care, apologies have a bad rep. Not long ago, if a doctor made a mistake while treating a patient, they were forbidden from discussing the error with the victim or the family. The implication was that a doctor must never to admit to anything that could end in a malpractice suit. As a result, generations of doctors adopted a cold, flat demeanor while delivering the news that a patient had died. Families might find out later a physician error was involved, but even then, the physician was discouraged from acting like a human being. To be sympathetic or express regret was to risk appearing to admit fault.

Eventually the medical profession came around, concluding that teaching young doctors the proper way to admit a medical error is not only ethically right, but also practical. In a 2004 article called "Disclosing Medical Error: A Professional Standard," researchers found that when physicians overcome their shame and fear of repercussion and promptly reported medical errors, they help to improve the safety and efficacy of the whole health care system. Doctors who apologize to the patient or the family often find that a sincere apology can actually comfort the family and lessen the desire to retaliate with a lawsuit.

CHAPTER 15
PROGRESS IS PERFECTION

———

IT'S MY FONDEST hope that by now you've undergone a change in your thinking, and quite possibly your behavior. Life is probably a little easier even though scanning your behavior for blunders is hard work. Making a formal apology to someone you care about is one thing, but it can stick in your throat with someone you don't care for. Either way, your apology skill is probably getting results.

Remember I promised that learning how to admit and correct your mistakes can have a ripple effect that could change the world? This is how we do it. Little by little, with one course correction, one admission of regret, one apology after another, you become a better person. So much better, in fact, you might even surprise yourself. You'll be less interested in getting your own point across, less focused on ducking responsibility or passing the blame for what you've done. When you come across others who are still operating the old way, you have more compassion because you used to be like them. Instead of pointing a finger at everyone else, you're standing tall.

Everyone makes mistakes, and now you understand this on a deeper level. In fact, the failure to acknowledge and accept this fact is just another mistake—the fundamental attribution error. Once you're "woke," going back to sleep is difficult. You can't forget what you know. The one who will suffer the most from the hurt of an unspoken apology, uncorrected mistake, or unrepaired damage is you. Like the fairy tale about the princess and the pea, even though your mistake is tiny and buried under twenty mattresses, you'll still feel it enough to keep you awake at night.

Congratulations. You're now on the side of the good guys. You're starting to be the change you'd like to see in the world. This skill can work for anyone, but knowing that it was you who started the ball rolling is important. Consider this: you might be the only example of a good apology that some people will ever see. Wear the mantle proudly.

And, if you backslide, remember the kind of person you want to be. A friend once told me, "I may not be in control of my first thought. But I do have control over the next one." I find this tremendously wise and reassuring. Of course, humans will continue to have impulses of which we're not proud of. We may even feel shame at discovering we're still capable to being rude, inconsiderate, mean, deceitful, or even downright bad.

There's no need for shame if you're trying to change. That means biting back harsh words, pausing before hitting "post," learning from mistakes, and trying again. In a life that can sometimes feel like a bumpy, scratchy scrabble through thickets, the good apology is healing medicine.

To err is human

Alice had been practicing the art of the good apology for a few years, and most of her relationships with family, friends, coworkers, and even strangers had improved. A quick, sincere apology for harm done had become a habit, and if she missed the boat now and then, her belly barometer would put her back on track.

One day at the supermarket she pulled into a tight parking space, and as she got out of her car, her door bumped against the side of a blue Ford pickup parked in the adjacent space. It seemed like nothing, so she went into the store. When she came out, there were two big guys standing by her car.

"You hit my car with your door." It wasn't a question, it was a challenge. The second guy piped in, "Yeah, I was sitting in his car when you did it."

Alice's heart raced. The size of the two guys, the rush she was in, and the fact that she knew she'd done what they were saying threw her off. She started to panic. She still hadn't said anything when the second guy added, "You really slammed it. You left a dent."

Now hold on a minute. Alice knew this was not true. Her door had barely tapped the second car, but the burden of proof was on her. She saw she had a choice; she could apologize the best way she knew how or fall back on her baser instincts. Alice opened her mouth to do the right thing, but baser instincts grabbed the mic and she said, "I don't know what you're talking about."

Alice knew full well that one lie always leads to another. She prided herself on being an honest person, a good person, and she'd been working so hard on her behavior, but in her panic she had jumped down the nearest rabbit hole, and she saw no other way out except further down.

Baser instincts gave the two guys attitude. "Do you have any proof, other than this man's hearsay?" she demanded. Alice hated her nasty tone. When the driver of the car didn't answer, Alice swept past him and got into her car. "I don't know what kind of scam you guys are trying to pull, but it's just not right. You shouldn't try to trick innocent people that way."

Oh, wow. Baser instincts dropped the mic. Alice pulled out of the parking space much faster than she intended, and one of the guys had to jump back. Her hands were sweating, and her heart was pounding so hard she thought she'd pass out, but all she could think about was getting the hell out of there.

Alice suffered over the incident for days, replaying it over and over in her mind. She was afraid to go to the same store for fear of running into one or both of the guys again. Every time she saw a dark blue Ford pickup, her anxiety went through the roof. She found no relief from her torment because she couldn't think of any way to make things right.

A nice, neat ending to this story would go great here—say, one in which Alice spots the two guys in a restaurant, screws up her courage, and approaches them to make her apology, thereby clearing her conscience and confirming her status as a do-the-right-thing kind of person, but it didn't happen that way. She never saw the guys in the pickup again, and gradually she got over the acute stages of guilt and the impulse to keep looking over her shoulder.

But the discomfort and sleepless nights taught Alice a lesson, and she resolved to do better. She recommitted to making her apology skill a way of life, which meant being prepared for the unexpected. Her experience also reinforced the difficult truth of the fundamental attribution error, which is that everyone sees the other person as the villain and themselves as the victim. To paraphrase my friend, we have little or no control over our first impulses, and first impulses are almost always negative. We do have control over what we do next, however, and this is where Alice now tries to do better. She's been known to say, even after a bad beginning, "Hold on, let me try this again. You're right. I did hit your car. I don't think it was hard enough to do any damage, but let's take a look."

Will some people try and take advantage of you? Yes, sometimes they will. But, you'll discover that people who will try to take advantage of your honest attempt to right a wrong are in the minority. As you may be finding out, most people rise nobly to the occasion, responding with more generosity and less anger. The law of karma states that the more you work on this part of your subtle superhero repertoire, the more you'll attract other decent, honest people, other superheroes.

Really what I'm trying to tell you is, be kind. I think most of us want that, to be kinder, to bring something positive to the world. It never hurts to look around and see how you can make things a little better than how you found them. That's my governing principle, and though it may not be yours, I'm asking you to think about it.

For reasons we haven't been able to fathom in thousands of years of human history and psychotherapy, human beings get off on being mean. Maybe it goes back to our oldest ancestors, who fought off both wild animals and neighboring tribes with the same ferocity, perceiving that both presented the same threats to survival. You're either going to eat me or my hard-won supply of food for the winter, which means I'll die if I don't kill you first.

The spectrum of good-to-evil thrives on social media, and no one knows this better than the post-Mario generation. Everyone knows of at least one story, whether from a news report, a meme, a flame war on a friend's feed, or a hallway conversation, about someone who died because of careless remarks, posts, or videos shared on social media. Facebook may be the mother ship but is by no means the only place where people are thoughtless, selfish, and mean. Cruelty online is so easy to justify, as the social scientists have pointed out, and it gives trolls the added advantage of being anonymous. It's all too easy to lose your inhibitions and join the feeding frenzy against someone you know only from their Tumblr.

There's a better way. Download any meditation app, and you're likely to see evidence that sages and poets and leaders all throughout history have been saying pretty much the same thing. Peace in the world starts with peace in the heart. For centuries, the leaders of the great wisdom traditions have insisted that it's possible to change human wiring. They've implored us to set aside the demons of our lower nature. They've demonstrated, through their own extraordinary goodness and self-sacrifice, that defusing conflict by giving others the benefit of the doubt and treating them with compassion and tolerance, instead of escalating it, is possible. That kind of person doesn't have to be a world-class sage. They can be an ordinary person like you or me.

EPILOGUE

In your life, in your relationships, in your everyday comings and goings, you have the power to make things better or to make them worse. Not just once in a lifetime, but dozens of times a day, in multiple situations. If you decide to adopt this simple practice, you will be challenged. Someone will push your buttons just the right way, or they'll take you by surprise when your guard is down. You'll meet someone who is relentless in their quest to destroy your peace of mind (or worse).

Until it becomes second nature, you're going to make mistakes. You may have to go back for a do-over, or you may have to rethink the whole enterprise with that person or that apology. The tools laid out in this book are simple, but this is no cakewalk. In most situations that require an honest, forthright apology, your heart will be pounding, and your brain will be barking orders. The person across from you may be freaking out, too, registering as a threat to your security, one that all your hardwiring will be telling you to fight, dominate, or avoid.

But you'll also find, as you try this out and observe the results, that it feels good to live this way. You can hold your head up and look yourself and other people in the eye, confident in your ability to live by your principles. Your principles are the truths in which you believe and by which you have decided to live. You have set your feet on a path that can take you somewhere amazing.

Being the kind of person who takes responsibility for their own humanity, faults and all, frees you from the compulsion to prove yourself to everyone. You will become more interested in the people around you and less interested in always getting your own way. You will know how be a calm, attentive presence for an angry or upset person, and you'll know how to respond in a way that can, not only resolve the problem at hand but also, move you into closer relationship. While you may not realize it right away, you will discover how to live the kind of life you've always wanted, in peaceful cooperation with those around you.

This is what a global community can look like, and this is where it starts. This is how to give to others, without even having to reach for the plastic or the loose change in your pocket. This is how to make the world better.

Try it. Use this tool well, and use it for life. And let me know how you're doing.

NOTES

Chapter 2

Cotton, Anthony. "The Need for Restorative Justice," The Wisconsin Law Journal | Commentary | Blogs | ON THE DEFENSIVE: The need for restorative justice, January 21, 2014. Available at: https://wislawjournal. com/2014/01/21/on-the-defensive-the-need-for-restorative-justice/

White, Brent T., *Say You're Sorry: Court-Ordered Apologies as a Civil Rights Remedy*, 91 Cornell L. Rev. 1261 (2006). Available at: http://scholarship.law.cornell.edu/clr/vol91/iss6/2

Wildes, Rabbi Mark. "How to Say Sorry: A Step-by-Step Guide for Yom Kippur," *The Blog of the Huffington Post*, 09/22/2015 04:40 pm ET, updated December 6, 2017. Available at: http://www.huffingtonpost.com/rabbi-mark-wildes/how-to-say-sorrythe-inte_b_8170340.html

Catholic Church. "The Sacrament of Penance and Reconciliation," in the *Catechism of the Catholic Church*, Part 2, Section 2, Chapter 2, Article 4. Available at: http://www.vatican.va/archive/ccc_css/archive/catechism/p2s2c2a4.htm.

Bhikkhu, Thanissaro. "Metta Means Goodwill." *Access to Insight (Legacy Edition),* November 24, 2013. Available at: http://www.accesstoinsight.org/lib/authors/thanissaro/metta_means_goodwill.html

Wikipedia Contributors. "Repentance." Wikipedia, the Free Encyclopedia. Accessed July 19, 2017. https://cn.wikipedia.org/wiki/Repentance.

Stinnett, Bill. "Leadership Means Never Having to Say You're Sorry." May 26, 2011. Available at: http://www.gordontraining.com/leadership/leadership-means-never-having-to-say-youre-sorry/#

Riley, Tonya. "Why a Starbucks Barista Has More Willpower Than You Do." *Heleo*, November 30, 2015. Available at: https://heleo.com/charles-duhigg-draft-how-starbucks-reversed-its-customer-service-rut/1050/

Chapter 3

Storms, Michael D. "Videotape and the attribution process: Reversing actors' and observers' points of view." *Journal of Personality and Social Psychology*, Vol 27/(2), August 1973, 165, 175.

Chapter 14

Bloom, J.D., Lauren M. *The Art of the Apology: How, When, and Why to Give and Accept Apologies*. Fine & Kahn, New York, 2008, 2014

Hobgood, M.D., Cherri, Hevin, M.D., Armando. "Disclosing Medical Error: A Professional Standard," Edited by Maurice R. Lemon, M.D., M.P.H. *Seminars in Medical Practice*, 2004, Vol 7, Turner-White Communications Inc. Available at: http://www.turner-white.com/memberfile.php?PubCode=smp_may04_error.pdf

ACKNOWLEDGMENTS

This book would not be possible without the support and contributions of steadfast friends and colleagues: my first readers James Dyer, Todd Witkin, Ethan Jacobi, Laura Collins, Lindsey Walaski, and Linda MacNeal; Kim Barron of New Leaf Design for the cover art and Alison Sheehy for the author photo; Julie Cottineau for inspiring me to take action and Mindy Gibbins-Klein for coaching me to the finish line; fellow editors Paul Fargis, Cynthia Read, Frances Jesson, and Sheila Buff for their support and advice; and all the beautiful friends and strangers who continually demonstrate the power of the human spirit to light the way to a more peaceful heart and a better world.

You have my deepest thanks.